BENT COPS

The Brighton Police conspiracy trial

David Rowland

𝓕𝓟

Finsbury Publishing

By the same author:
On the Brighton Beat: stories about Brighton Police
War in the City, volumes I and II
The Brighton Blitz
The Coastal Blitz
Spitfires Over Sussex: the exploits of 602 Squadron
Out of the Blue: the story of Brighton's worst air attack
Survivors: aircrew stories of World War II

British Library Cataloguing-in Publication Data.
A catalogue record for this book is available from the British Library.

ISBN 978-0-9539392-7 5

Published by Finsbury Publishing, 2 Harvest Close, Telscombe Cliffs,
Peacehaven, East Sussex BN10 7JG

Dedication

To Frank Knight and Ray Hovey

I have known Frank Knight and Ray Hovey for many years, both being ex-colleagues of mine in the Brighton Borough Police Force.

Frank Knight spent a number of years in the CID and the plain clothes department, both as a constable and as a sergeant. In the 1970s I worked with him in the Brighton communications room at John Street. He was one of the most 'laid back' officers I have ever worked with – an attribute not to be confused with laziness or being uncaring. When there was an incident running Frank would calmly roll a cigarette before taking charge of the incident and bringing it to a satisfactory conclusion.

He was without doubt one of the nicest people you could ever wish to meet. He was a man's man who didn't suffer fools gladly. I

really did enjoy working with him in a police environment as you were always sure of a fun shift, whatever was going on. He had the greatest respect for his colleagues of all ranks and would put himself out to help others.

Ray Hovey spent almost the whole of his police career in the CID, where he became a detective sergeant. As with Frank, it was always a fun time when you were in his company. During the many social occasions at John Street

The late Frank Knight on duty on the lower esplanade at the bottom of West Street. [Moya Knight]

police station Ray would be the life and soul of the party. He had a very distinctive laugh which could be heard a mile away.

I got to know Ray more after we retired from the police force and both worked in the security department at the Brighton Co-op in London Road. He was the deputy security officer, and he interviewed me for the job.

It took great courage for these two men to appear as witnesses for the prosecution against more senior policemen in the Brighton Police conspiracy trial. They both stood for honesty and integrity, and proved as much in one of the highest courts in the land, the Old Bailey.

Ray Hovey. [Rene Hovey]

Both in the days leading up to the trial in Brighton and in its aftermath, local police officers had a very tough time with some members of the public, but like all good forces they managed to weather the storm and became stronger for the experience. Indeed, after this terrible case the Brighton force went on to be one of the best and most efficient in the country.

It is my pleasure to dedicate this book to two proud and wonderful officers who policed the town with fairness and devotion.

Acknowledgements

My thanks to Moya Knight, who has helped me considerably by supplying information about her husband and the trial in general, and to Ray Hovey, who was also of great assistance, both verbal and documentary.

And a special mention to my grandson, Elliot Hogan, for his technical expertise.

Contents

POLICE

THINGS

en Property :
in Contact

ORTER

grocer and self-
said in evidence
esterday that he
ficers about £250
nsp. Hammersley
bout £50."

gt. TREVOR HEATH, and
ef Constable, with two
Waite, dark-haired and
t and maroon bow tie,

They also had meat and
ngs.

OWARD: Did they pay for
gs they had each week?—
sed to have two or three
orth of stuff, give me a 10s
i wait for the change.
used to ask for change: they
ver asked for change: they
or it.
if he could give an estimate
much money he had given
to Hammersley, WAITE re-
" It is difficult to say over a
Round about £200." It
e " very difficult " to tell the
f the other things he had.
said he had given to Heath
£50."

HOWARD: Did you ever give
oney to Mr. Ridge?—Not per-
sir.
d if he had ever had goods
Nescafe, Waite said: " Yes."
erred to some stolen Nescafe,
id he had a conversation with
ersey and Heath after his
al

The Accused &
The Charges

The accused are:

Charles Field Williams Ridge,
58, suspended Chief Constable
of Brighton, Bavant Road,
Brighton.

John Richard Hamm__ 39,
who, as a chief inspe__ was
second in command of __righ-
ton C.I.D., of Glen Ride, Withdean, Brighton.

Trevor Ernest Heath, 35, a detective sergeant in Brighton
C.I.D., of Bramble Rise, Withdean, Brighton.

Anthony John Lyons, 59, licensee, of Marine Gate, Brighton.

Samuel Bellson, 42, bookmaker,
The Drive, Hove.

All five are charged with having between Jan. 1, 1948, and
Oct. 18, 1957, conspired together
and with other persons unknown
corruptly to solicit and obtain rewards for Heath, Hammersley
and Ridge, for showing or promis-
ing favours contrary to their duty
as police officers and thereby to
obstruct and defeat the course of
public justice.

Heath was also charged with
being a person serving under the
Crown he attempted on June 27,
1957, to obtain from Alan Roy
Bennett (formerly known as
Brown) £50 as a reward for showing favour to him in relation to
the affairs of the Crown.

---

load was delivered, WAITE said: " He
used to come to the shop. The shop
in New England Road was open
then."

Hammersley made a report about
the peaches, said Waite, and two of
the men working for him were taken
to the Town Hall and questioned
about them.

Mr. HOWARD: Were any proceedings taken against you?—There were
going to be proceedings taken
against me—Have any proceedings
been taken against you?—No, Sir.

Waite said that on August Bank
Holiday Saturday this year he saw a

---

asked. in cross-exam__
green dye Ministry of Food off
put on meat unfit for human
sumption. Waite replied that
was on the meat the enforce
officer did not bother to look.

Mr. BOSLEY: Do you reme
saying " there were going to be
ceedings against me but Sco
Yard came in "?—I said I th
there would be proceedings.
not charged. Mr. Hamm
wanted me prosecuted.

You have read the newspap
ports?—Yes, very good report

Did you read what the So
General described you as?—
heard very well.

Did the Solicitor-General s
were a greengrocer, fruiter
poulterer, an undischarged
rupt, a receiver of stolen goo
obviously a scoundrel?

CROWN OBJECTIO
Not in Court

Mr. MAXWELL TURNER,
prosecution, objected, sayin
cannot know what the S
General said about him. He
in court. He can only say
has read in the papers what
about him."

Mr. BOSLEY: Is it corre
that you read the papers ab
the Solicitor-General said a
—I never read it. I was
many people I did not ha
it.

When you heard what p
did you not then look at
yourself?—No. I was too

I see you are smiling
that. Would the Solici
be wrong in describing
greengrocer, fruiterer and
—No. I don't think so.

Would he be wrong
scribed you as an u
bankrupt?—You should
Mr. Bosley. You are
acting for the trustees.

Mr. Bosley referred
tion " and Waite replied
once my solicitor."

Mr. W. H. VOKINS,
asked Waite to answer

Mr. BOSLEY: Would
General be wrong in
as a receiver of stolen
can he be wrong?

6

The Story Breaks

The first news of a bribery probe involving Brighton police hit the headlines on Wednesday 2nd October, 1957. At a press conference in the town hall the chief constable, Charles Ridge, disclosed that at his request Scotland Yard had been called in to investigate 'certain allegations of irregularities' in the Brighton police force.

He admitted that these investigations had been going on for about a month but that no member of the force had been suspended.

That afternoon an emergency meeting was called by the watch committee. Fourteen members met for about 35 minutes in a second-floor committee room at the town hall. A large number of journalists had gathered outside, and they were admitted once the meeting was over. It had been chaired by Councillor George Baldwin. To his left sat the town clerk, Mr. W.O. Dodd, and behind them stood the chief constable in his full dress uniform.

The clerk stood to read out a prepared statement on behalf of the committee: 'We have been informed by the town clerk and the chief constable that investigations are being conducted by officers of the Metropolitan Police Force concerning suggested bribery and corruption affecting a member of the Brighton Police Force. Until the results of the investigations are complete and made known to the committee they do not expect to be in possession of any further information.'

A brief pause was followed by a barrage of questions from the gathered pressmen, the first being asked by a crime reporter from London. Was there really only one member of the force involved, he asked, and if so, why should ten Scotland Yard officers be called in?

'I cannot comment on the methods used by Scotland Yard' Dodd answered, 'and would advise the chief constable also not to comment.'

The reporters were unsatisfied with the answer just given, but Dodd continuing to play a dead bat.

'I cannot forecast what the investigations will produce,' he said. 'Bribery and corruption sometimes spread.'

One reporter asked if it was known to the committee that a man serving a sentence for fraud had made a statement saying that he had paid money over a period of years to a member of the Brighton police force.

'I can neither confirm nor deny this,' was the reply. 'I don't know.'

A question was then asked about the identity of the officer being investigated.

'I do not know who it is or what rank he holds,' Dodd told him, 'and no action has been taken until the investigations show justification for such action.'

Later Dodd confirmed that the watch committee had known nothing about the investigations until that morning.

'The only people in Brighton to know about them are the chief constable and myself, who knew from their inception.'

He added that publicity at the outset would have probably hampered the investigations. Councillor Baldwin, who had little to say throughout the questioning, added, 'I have no idea of the identity of the man concerned in the statement. We in Brighton are completely in the dark. It is absolutely true. We have no information or contact with Scotland Yard. I didn't know, and neither did my committee, that these investigations were going on.'

In fact rumours and counter rumours had been circulating for many months throughout Brighton about senior policemen accepting bribes. Other rumours centred on 'call girl' and large scale corruption rackets. The chief constable had done his best to dispel these rumours, as had members of the watch committee.

On Friday 4th October the town clerk issued a fuller statement on the ongoing investigations.

'I have not seen a single member of the Scotland Yard investigation squad,' he said, 'and I do not know from where they are taking statements. As they have been called in by the chief constable to investigate an allegation of bribery affecting the force here in Brighton, that is their job, and that only until they are directed to something else.

'I was astounded to read a statement in one newspaper alleging that businessmen were paying for favours from town officials. Had

I the slightest suspicion that any of my colleagues had been so conducting themselves; I should immediately have taken appropriate action. I am not aware of any inquiry by Scotland Yard or anyone else concerning the town's officials, and I should expect to have been informed at a very early stage if such inquiries were afoot.'

Dodd then referred to a particular allegation of corruption involving the council.

'So far, where the so-called "land grab" is concerned, I know that everything my council did was done legally and openly and indeed was the subject of a complete statement in the agenda of the council. The decision to sell privately was taken following the

Chief Constable Charles Ridge, photographed in 1956, the year before the allegations of police corruption.

government's change of policy and the price for sale of the plots that were sold was fixed by the council on the advice of the valuer and with the approval of the district valuer, and the plots were openly offered for sale. For the reputation of the town, for its good order and government, I hope and have every confidence that the enquiry will be thorough and speedy.'

On the same day Councillor Baldwin attended a police prize-giving event held at Wellington Road police station. During his speech he told officers that 'It would be wise to ignore rumours, sensationalism and wild conjecture that have taken place in the press, and await the result of these investigations. It would be wholly unjust to damn the many for acts by possibly the few. From my enquiries I can assure the public that they can repose their full confidence in the police force of Brighton, and in the thoroughness of their investigations.'

The watch committee held a two and a half hour closed meeting on Wednesday 9th October. Afterwards the town clerk said that the allegations were a matter purely for the police, and that the committee did not wish to comment further until the investigations had been completed. He told waiting journalists that he had received a letter from the director of public prosecutions. It was a reply to his letter about the probe, in which he had raised the fact that it had been leaked to the press before the committee had been informed of it. He then read out the contents of the letter:

'I am in receipt of your letter of the 2nd instant and I can assure you that the information that has appeared in the press did not in any way come from this department. Further, I am informed by the Commissioner of the Metropolitan Police that no statement to the press has been made by his department. I am sure that you will readily appreciate that the appearance of Metropolitan Police officers in any town outside London is frequently a matter of interest, comment and speculation by the press.'

The senior Scotland Yard officer leading the investigation was Detective Superintendent Ian Forbes-Leith. He was acting under the direct orders of Commander George Hatherill, head of the CID at Scotland Yard. On Wednesday 9th and Thursday 10th October the two men interviewed the chief constable. On the second day the Brighton solicitor John Bosley spent about 20 minutes in Ridge's office. When the local press asked him about his visit, he replied, 'I often call at the town hall,' and left without saying more.

Later in the afternoon it was announced that officers from the Brighton force were assisting Scotland Yard with their enquiry. Four officers were interviewed in Lewes by members of the Yard's investigating squad, who were now based there. No names or other information were given, and immediately after the interviews they returned to Brighton and resumed their normal duties.

Now the Brighton MP Howard Johnson became involved. He asked a Scotland Yard officer to see him, and passed him evidence that had come into his possession. An anonymous caller to his office had given him information about the payment of money to a businessman in Lewes Road.

The Arrests

On Thursday 17th October two Brighton magistrates were asked to be at the town hall at 9 o'clock the following meeting. A decision had been taken that a Brighton officer should be arrested.

At 10.20 am a black car carrying Commander Hatherill and Superintendent Forbes-Leith drew up outside the main entrance. The two officers were immediately shown into the chief constable's office. A second car brought other Scotland Yard officers, including Detective Inspector Butler, Detective Inspector Mitchell, Detective Sergeant Barnett and Detective Sergeant Vibart. They waited in an ante-room.

A few minutes later Inspector Butler was called in. Detective Sergeant Trevor Heath was sent for, and then his solicitor, Mr. Wheeler and Superintendent Williams, head of Brighton CID, joined the meeting. Heath was arrested on a warrant signed by the two local magistrates.

The town clerk issued a statement announcing Heath's arrest, adding that the chief constable had suspended him from duty immediately. Heath and the two senior Scotland Yard officers crossed the road to the CID office, where Heath had his fingerprints taken. About twenty minutes later they returned to the chief constable's office.

Enter the Yard: Det Ch Insp Ernie Millen, who made arrests in Brighton.

A short time later Forbes-Leith and Butler drove Heath and his solicitor in a Yard car to Heath's bungalow at 58 Bramble Drive, Withdean. His wife, ten-year-old son Rodney and six-year-old daughter Barbara were not at home during the 40 minutes they spent inside.

They returned to the town hall at about midday, and at 12.25 pm Heath appeared in court. At the hearing, his solicitor stated that Heath had allowed his home to be searched without a warrant.

Only a few members of the public were present during the 15-minute hearing, but the public benches were filled with reporters, anxious not to miss any small grain of information.

The charge against Trevor Heath was read out to him, 'that being a person serving under the Crown, he attempted to obtain £50 in June from Alan Roy Bennett as a reward for showing favour to the said Alan Roy Bennett in relation to affairs of the Crown, contrary to the Prevention of Corruption Act 1906.'

Det Supt Forbes-Leith, the only witness, said that he had seen Heath in the chief constable's office earlier that day and had read the warrant to him.

After being cautioned, Heath replied, 'It's a fantastic allegation. I have said before he has a reason for making such allegations against me.'

The superintendent asked the magistrates that he be remanded in custody, but his solicitor made a strong plea for bail. He stated that Trevor Heath had been a member of Brighton Police for a long time, the last 10 years being in the CID. The superintendent

The Brighton CID offices in Market Street, opposite the town hall, at the time of the trial. The police canteen was in the basement.

strongly opposed bail, giving four reasons for his objection, and the magistrates decided to remand Heath in custody.

Just before ten 'clock on the morning of Friday 25th October, a secret meeting and a handshake on the seafront began a day of truly momentous events – one of the worst in the history of Brighton Police. They would soon be famous the world over, but for all the wrong reasons. Within five hours of this handshake the Scotland Yard investigating officers would swoop and make three arrests, two of them truly shocking for the local force.

The seafront meeting took place opposite the Old Ship Hotel. Commander George Hatherill and Det Supt Forbes-Leith had driven down from London that morning. Hatherill walked up to a bowler-hatted man who was leaning on the railings looking out to sea and clapped him on the shoulder. This was Sir William Johnson, one of her majesty's inspectors of constabulary. The men shook hands and exchanged a few words before climbing into a Scotland Yard car and driving the few hundred yards to the town hall.

Chief Constable Charles Ridge was in his office with Det Chief Insp Radford, another of the Yard's officers, and the deputy head of Brighton CID, Det Insp John Hammersley, who had walked, smiling, across the road from his CID headquarters only minutes before. At about 10.45 Forbes-Leith walked in – and promptly arrested both Ridge and Hammersley.

The chief constable, in reply to the charge, said, 'It is absolutely preposterous,' while Hammersley said, 'I deny the allegations.'

At 11.05 there was a further arrest: Anthony Lyons, the owner of Sherry's Bar in West Street. Det Ch Insp Ernie Millen formally charged him just after midday. When he was charged he made no reply. They had all been charged with conspiracy and would appear in court together.

Soon afterwards Commander Hatherill and Sir William Johnson attended a special meeting of the watch committee at the town hall. After 28 minutes it was announced that the chief constable was being suspended, together with Det Insp Hammersley.

The chairman of the watch committee announced that the deputy chief constable, Supt T. Hill, would be the caretaker chief, responsible for the day-to-day running of the force until another chief constable was appointed – possibly as early as the following week.

At 12.45pm the magistrates, Mr. W. Vokins (chairman), Mrs Elizabeth Dacre and Colonel S. Lynn, took their places in the court room. Chief Constable Ridge stood stern-faced in the middle, with Hammersley standing on his right and Lyons on his left. They stood almost to attention while the clerk of the court read out the charge: 'it is alleged that between January 1st 1948 and October 18th 1957 they conspired together with other persons unknown corruptly to solicit and obtain rewards for Trevor Ernest Heath, John Richard Hammersley and Charles Field Williams Ridge, for showing favours contrary to their duty and thereby obstructing the course of public justice.'

Mr. R. Thomas, for the director of public prosecutions, said that it was not yet possible to proceed with the case as there were further

Brighton town hall. The police station and cells were in the basement, and now house a police museum.

enquiries to be made. After some deliberation the magistrates remanded all three in custody.

A crowd of nearly 400 people had gathered hoping to get a glimpse of the arrested officers. However, the police had a plan whereby they would get the defendants away quickly and out of the public gaze. An elaborate decoy was staged in order to execute their plan.

After the court hearing, the crowd massed in front of the police station in Bartholomews, where it was believed the three defendants would be leaving from. At 3 o'clock precisely a 'black maria' driven by a policewoman nosed its way through the crowd, sounding its horn and forcing its way to the entrance of the police station. Behind it came an escorting patrol car. The crowd surged forward when they saw these two vehicles, convinced that the defendants would soon be getting into the back of the van. The uniformed policemen held the onlookers back, making a pathway from the van to the police station doorway.

Scores of photographers surged forward, cameras at the ready, while newsreel cameramen rushed to any vantage point they could reach. One stood on a car bumper to gain some height.

Meanwhile at the other side of the town hall, a large black saloon and a patrol car driven by a plain clothes policeman slid quietly to a halt outside the rear entrance, the engines still running. Only a handful of people saw the three defendants and their escorts leave the building. The chief constable was the first out and paused for a second before stepping into the waiting vehicle. Lyons came out second and covered his face with his coat. Hammersley, who just before leaving had shaken hands with several police colleagues, got into the second vehicle.

They were quickly driven away, but not before another police car had been drawn across the junction of Market Street and Prince Albert Street to ensure that they would not be hindered or followed. The crowd eventually began to disperse, and the police station was left to carry on with its everyday duties.

At 10.40 am on Tuesday 12th November Scotland Yard officers arrested Samuel Bellson, a 42-year-old bookmaker of 85a Drive

Court, The Drive in Hove. He was the fifth and final person to be arrested and charged.

He was arrested at his home by Det Supt Forbes-Leith and Det Ch Insp Ernie Millen. When charged at the police station he made no reply. He was bailed in his own surety of £100 and another in the same amount, provided by Isaac Bendom of Astra House, Kings Road in Brighton.

It was announced that he would appear at court with the other four accused on 25th November.

New Brooms

On Monday 28th October Exeter's chief constable, Albert Rowsell, arrived in Brighton as the temporary chief constable. At 5 pm a special meeting of Brighton's watch committee was convened in order that all its members could meet Mr. Rowsell. He informed them that he had been in charge at Exeter since 1941, having joined their force in 1919.

On the same day Det Supt Forbes-Leith moved his office from Lewes to Brighton. He was given a room on the top floor of the town hall, normally used for committee meetings. At 9.25 am he and an assistant arrived, each carrying a suitcase and a brief case. Other members of the team were working from an office next to the typists' office in the CID headquarters.

Albert Rowsell became Brighton's new police chief.

Rowsell made his first appearance the following day, and it was not the smoothest of beginnings. He was in the ante-room of the council chamber and talking to the mayor, Alderman Charles Tyson, the chairman of the watch committee, George Baldwin, and the town clerk, W.O. Dodd.

The room was packed with reporters and photographers all vying to get a good position. The flash bulbs of the cameras continued to light up the room for almost two minutes, causing a barrage of brilliant light, and Rowsell decided that he had had enough. He turned his back on some of the photographers, then suddenly turned around and said, 'No more pictures, please.'

Some photographers protested that they hadn't been able to get their pictures. Rowsell, by now quite rattled, said, 'If you want my co-operation, do as I ask and cut it out.' He then walked out of the room leaving Cllr Baldwin to explain the circumstances to the angry pressmen.

Bill Cavey, the new CID chief in Brighton, would later become the town's last chief constable.

A number of the reporters started to ask questions, and Baldwin said that he would answer what he could. His first answer caused the reporters to scribble frantically on their note pads: Rowsell would get a higher salary than Ridge had got, a figure of £2,100 compared with £1.900, because he was already on a higher grade at Exeter.

He also confirmed that the three police officers under arrest were suspended on two-thirds pay.

There was soon news of another newcomer from Exeter. On Wednesday 13th November the watch committee made a surprise announcement when they promoted the 42-year-old William Cavey, a detective inspector in Devon, to detective superintendent in charge of Brighton CID. He took over from Det Supt Gwyn Williams, who was on sick leave in his native South Wales and would not be allowed to return to the CID if he returned to duty.

Dodd was questioned about the appointment of an officer to a post while it was still officially held by another officer. He replied that it was not unusual under the circumstances, as Williams was seriously ill, suffering from mental exhaustion and would soon be eligible for retirement.

Bill Cavey had been a police officer for 22 years and head of the CID in Exeter since his promotion to inspector in 1953. During the war he had served as a Fleet Air Arm pilot and was stationed for a short while at Courtenay Gate in Hove, then a naval establishment.

He was destined to become the 13th and the final chief constable of Brighton Police.

Tension Mounts

During the second week of November, with the trial of the five men getting ever closer, an air of great excitement was building in the town. It seemed that the forthcoming trial was the only topic of conversation in pubs and workplaces.

The newsmen were continually buzzing around, anxious to glean any little scrap of information they could. The local papers of course wanted to be the first with any important news about the trial. A *Brighton and Hove Herald* headline on Saturday 23rd November read, '60 witnesses may be called in 12-day hearing'.

Headlines such as this sparked off further debate about the trial and who would be involved. The court would be sitting for almost two weeks, and the defence lawyers caused great consternation by announcing that they would ask magistrates to ban the press from the court room. It was firmly believed, however, that they would never agree to this, and that the whole session would be conducted in open court.

The town was thus set for the biggest court case in the history of the town, with fervent interest spreading beyond Britain to many countries abroad.

On Friday 1st November a queen's counsel, a barrister and four solicitors prepared to make strong pleas for bail in the police conspiracy case at Brighton magistrates court. They arrived at the main door of the town hall, their brief cases bulging with important papers. They expected a battle with the prosecution team who they believed were going to oppose it.

A little earlier, at 10.25 am, Ridge had arrived almost unnoticed in a pre-war car. The two detectives and Lyons had got there about half an hour before him and were detained in the cell block.

More than a hundred members of the public had queued for a long time to get in, some bringing their knitting, others sitting patiently on the town hall steps.

The defence team were to receive a surprise, as Mr. R. Thomas, for the director of public prosecutions, said there would be no objection to bail for all the defendants involved – adding that Scotland Yard had reached a stage in their inquires where they did not need to oppose it. All the defendants were therefore remanded on bail until Monday 25th November.

The magistrates renewed the bail of £500 that had been granted to Charles Ridge the previous Wednesday by a judge in chambers. This was in his own surety of £250 and another from his married daughter, Mrs. Elizabeth Wiffin, of the same amount.

The two CID officers and Mr. Lyons were each granted bail in their own recognisance for £100, and a surety each for the same amount. Lyons' surety was a licensee, Solomon Rubenstein of Cambridge Heath Road in London.

Mr. H. Cushnie MBE, the magistrates' chairman, then warned the defendants against interfering with the witnesses. The hearing had lasted just 17 minutes.

Ridge was driven away accompanied by his daughter and his solicitor. He smiled and waved to the crowd as some of them shouted out, 'Good luck!' Next to leave was Lyons, who used a brown paper bag to hide his face from photographers. Just before one o'clock the two detectives left, having had to wait until their sureties had appeared and had been approved by the magistrates.

Mrs Elsie Astbury of Sussex Square stood bail for Trevor Heath, while Hedley Walter Moffatt, a Brighton hotelier of Atlingworth Street, stood bail for John Hammersley.

Miss Betty Laskey, a 25-year old secretary, was the only person who knew everything about the case before it reached the Brighton court. She had more than a million words dictated to her by various members of the team. Her work being highly secret, she was taken everywhere by a Scotland Yard car and never left the town hall without a police escort.

Special precautions had been taken to safeguard the room's contents. The Yard men had a special new type of lock fitted to the door, which was padlocked every night when they left. Senior officers of the investigation team kept the keys on their person.

The Trial: Day One

Sixty six-year-old Mrs. Christine Knowles of 9a Eaton Place was first in the queue that formed outside the town hall for the opening of the conspiracy trial on Monday 25th November. She arrived at 7am, taking up her position outside the western entrance. The court eventually opened at 10.40, and there was a queue of more than 50 people for the public gallery.

At 10 o'clock a Scotland Yard car was at Brighton station to meet the four men presenting the case for the prosecution: the solicitor general, Sir Harry Hylton-Foster, Mr. J. Maxwell Turner, Mr. Gerald Howard QC and Mr. Ryland Thomas .

At 10.26 Trevor Heath arrived for the hearing dressed in a smart grey suit and a red and black tie. He was closely followed by Commander George Hatherill, who had led the investigation from his London office. Within the next few minutes the other

CID officers in the dock: John Hammersley (left) and Trevor Heath pictured on their way to Brighton magistrates court. [Author's collection]

defendants arrived. Charles Ridge stopped outside the town hall, shook hands and chatted to a number of journalists.

With the magistrates in their places, the defendants entered the court room and the scene was set for perhaps the biggest case in Brighton's long and colourful history. On trial were the three police officers, the bookmaker Samuel Bellson and the bar manager Anthony Lyons.

As the court convened, Cyril Weaver, the solicitor acting for Heath, stood up and addressed the magistrates. He wanted to know how the second charge against his client would be addressed, and was politely informed that all the evidence would be heard together. Mr Wheeler, not content with the answer, said that he failed to understand this, suggesting that either it should be heard separately or the charge should be dismissed. After further discussion, the chairman of the court, Howard Vokins, told him, 'We will hear all the evidence first.'

Opening the case for the Crown, Sir Harry warned that much of the evidence he would call came from people 'generally described as shady sources', and not from the best people. Those involved in a conspiracy were often 'people who break the criminal law and want to prevent the impact of justice . . . so therefore, I submit, it would be most unwise for anyone to form any conclusion about this case until the matter has been fully tried out.'

He told the magistrates that an incident involved Hammersley, Bellson and a former police officer named Barnard, who was invalided out of the force in 1952 and became an inquiry agent. In the course of his work Barnard had to serve writs, and in August 1953 he had to serve one on Bellson. Barnard knew that Bellson would be in court on 3rd August, so he went there and saw Trevor Heath, who pointed Bellson out to him. Barnard followed Bellson down the road and served his writ.

A few days later Barnard was driving down a hill when he saw he was being followed by a police car. He stopped and went into a public house and waited in the private bar.

Hammersley came in with another officer. The other officer then moved away from them. Hammersley mentioned that Barnard had served the writ on Bellson and used information he had obtained from Heath. Sir Harry alleged that Hammersley then said to Barnard, 'Watch your step. We have to look after Sammy Bellson. You had better keep your mouth shut.' He also alleged that Hammersley became threatening and said they would fix or frame Barnard if he did not.

Sir Harry went on to tell the magistrates of another incident, which he said involved two men named Leach. They were father and son, and the older, aged 64 years, was a wholesale fish merchant, while his son John, aged 40 years, owned fish shops.

In 1951 the son started running a drinking club next door to one of his fish shops at 74a West Street. He called it the Burlesque Club, his father and others had a financial interest in the club. In 1954, John Leach loaned some money to one of his customers on security of three watches and a travelling clock. The man to whom he loaned the money was Michael Roberts, who Sir Harry alleged, was 'a young thief'. Roberts was unable to redeem the articles and later, with another man named Mitchell – who Sir Harry said was also a young thief – broke into a shop. Subsequently the younger Leach bought some objects. Then came a visit from Hammersley and Heath. They asked John Leach about the purchases and Leach described Roberts very well and admitted the purchases. The officers called again the next day and took away some of the objects. They arranged to come again later and did so, and the younger Leach handed over some more articles he had got from the two men.

Bellson arrived on the scene by paying a visit to the home of the older Leach, when John Leach was also present. Sir Harry alleged that Bellson said, 'This case can be straightened out, you know. Shall I try and do it for you?' The older Leach gave Bellson £50, but he came back half an hour later, put the £50 on the table and said, 'It's not enough.' The older Leach asked 'What do they want?'

Sir Harry said, 'Nothing was said about the police force, but it was understood that "they" were the police.' The older Leach took out another £50 and handed it to Bellson, who was away again for half an hour and returned. Once more, it was not enough.

Bellson said, 'I put it on the desk and he just laughed at me,' stated Sir Harry.

On the same day, or maybe the following day, Charles Ridge, then a detective superintendent, called on the older Leach. Again John Leach was present, but Ridge said that he wanted to see his father – privately. John Leach left and a conversation then ensued. Ridge appeared to feel sorry for Leach senior, saying that he was really sorry that his son had got into trouble. Leach said, 'All I can ask is that you do the best you can for him.'

Ridge got up from his chair and as he was leaving said 'Whatever you do, Harry, keep in with the law' or 'keep within the law'. Mr Leach couldn't remember the exact words.

A little later Hammersley met John Leach and he said, 'If you have to go to court you will have to have a solicitor and maybe a barrister and that may cost you £300 to £400.' John Leach said, 'What can I do?' Hammersley replied, 'Well for £250 the evidence can be taken down and slung in the sea.' This annoyed Leach.

Later John Leach appeared in court and was convicted by the magistrates but had the conviction quashed on appeal to quarter sessions. He was awarded costs against the police.

Sir Harry said that after the inquiries had been started in Brighton, Scotland Yard officers saw Samuel Bellson and asked him if he would care to tell them of any dealings with the police force. Bellson said, 'I could tell you a lot, I will help you all I can.' Bellson then said to them, 'There is someone else you ought to see, that is old Harry Leach who lives in Stanford Avenue. They did his son over some jewellery. Ridge sent me along to do some business for him, but Leach would not pay enough and later Ridge went himself.'

Sir Harry then referred to the man Bennett, mentioned in the charge against Trevor Heath. He said he was known by several names. He had married a Norwegian lady and they had bought the Astor Hotel in Kings Road and converted the basement into a drinking club, known as the Astor Club. This club opened at Easter 1955 and was run by Bennett, who at that time was known as Brown. Lyons, who was an old friend, visited Brown and said it was possible to serve drinks all night without being bothered by anyone. Brown left Lyons to make the arrangements and soon after he took Ridge to the club and introduced him. Mrs. Brown was present, and Lyons and Brown in the hearing of Ridge proceeded to discuss how much Ridge would have to be paid. They fixed on 'a score' [£20] a week.

Ridge expressed some admiration of Brown's Jaguar car and said 'My wife likes nice things.' Brown said, 'Don't worry, it will be looked after.'

Sir Harry then went on to explain about the club, saying that the place was illegally run. Drinks were sold night after night until two or three in the morning. It was a drunken place, a noisy place and there were many fights. It became well known as 'The Bucket of Blood.'

Ridge made several visits there, usually at weekly intervals, and Brown gave him £20 on about five occasions. The payments were made in £5 notes. The last of these payments was made at Sherry's bar, where Ridge used to drink at one end of the bar where the manager's friends drank. It appears to have been known as 'Tattersalls'. On that occasion the notes were put into a newspaper and then handed to him. That was the last payment made to Ridge personally.

Soon after that Trevor Heath called at the reception office and asked to see Brown alone. Heath told him, 'From now on I will be calling for the presents from the club.' When Brown asked if Ridge had sent him, Heath replied, 'Yes, I will be calling in future.'

Heath called regularly after that and was given four £5 notes. If Brown could not be present, the money was put in an envelope and left behind the counter and handed to him by Mrs. Brown or the barmaid.

After some meetings they got to know one another rather well and Brown called Heath 'Trevor'. Once when he collected the money, Brown said to him, 'Do you get your whack out of the £20?' Heath shrugged his shoulders and said, 'A few pounds.'

After that Brown gave him occasionally in addition to the £20 for Ridge, £5 for himself. Once they went to London together and Brown bought him some ties. A number of ties were found when

Heath's home was searched. They got on very well together until one day when Ridge and Heath found out that Brown had a police record and Heath produced a photograph of Brown. Brown looked at it and said, 'That was about 10 years ago; I am a businessman now.' Brown continued to pay the money, week by week.

While Sir Harry was addressing the court, the five defendants were busy making notes on their writing pads. He continued that Heath had telephoned the club when the Brighton police were 'doing their rounds'. (Visiting licensed premises.)

He next referred to a Mrs. Cherryman, who was a receptionist at the club. She got a little frightened lest she might be involved. In fact she went to the police and ultimately saw Ridge. She spoke to him about a letter, and then asked to speak with him alone, saying, 'I don't know who to trust in the CID.' She told Ridge that the club was open until the early hours, and one night she had a telephone call by a man who said, 'Tell Alan to close the club tonight. Tell him it is Charlie.'

Sir Harry spoke of a man named Walker, who went to the club and who was arrested. Heath went back to the hotel later because Walker had said that £1,000 had gone from his bedroom. He persisted that Brown must have had the money and that 'the police wanted their whack'. Sir Harry said, 'That ended with Brown handing over money. Fortunately, in the interests of justice, Mrs. Brown heard some of this conversation. Later on, Heath asked to see Brown privately and told him that there was an inquiry from Leeds.'

Brown said that it was not possible for him to travel to Leeds, as it was the height of the season. Heath retorted that if Leeds police wanted him to go, then he would go.

Sir Harry said that this matter was 'squared up' by Brown giving Heath £15 or £20, and Brown heard nothing more about the Leeds enquiry.

In September Heath came again to see Brown saying that he wanted to buy a car, but he didn't quite have enough money to pay the deposit. Brown gave him £70 in part exchange for some rings. Up to that time Brown had made about 15 weekly payments to

Heath of £15–£20 and the club had never been raided despite the conduct of the premises. Shortly after this visit by Heath, Brown decided to take a holiday and then to close the club.

In June 1956, Mrs. Mason took over the club, but she observed the licensed rules and didn't serve after hours or to non-members.

One day Lyons paid her a visit saying that Brown had someone at the police station who tipped him off when the police were coming. On this information he always closed down the club. He strongly indicated that she could have the same arrangement and that he would want £5 a week each for the two of them. He told her that if she paid, she could do whatever she liked, serve after hours, especially on Sunday afternoons, and she would then be covered.

She quickly decided that she would have nothing to do with any such arrangements. One day Mrs. Mason's daughter, Mrs. Newman, was serving at the bar when Lyons came in bringing some visitors. She handed him the visitors' book. Lyons said, 'Do me a favour, take that away.' Lyons called again and told Mrs. Mason that she was being very silly.

The club was raided in July and she was fined for serving non-members. Mrs. Mason complained about it being unfair: she got caught while others didn't. Lyons said that Brown was more fortunate and got a tip when the police were coming.

Later, when Lyons was seen by the police he said that he knew the club was running after hours, but so were many others. He said he thought he might have taken Ridge there. He also thought that he might have introduced him to Brown, but he denied that payments were arranged or any were received.

When Heath was interviewed, he said he had only been to the club on two occasions and that it was quite untrue that he had visited the club weekly. When, during the interview, he was accused of receiving £20 weekly for the protection of the club he said, 'That is fantastic, what protection can I give?' He was then told that he was sent there by the then Detective Superintendent Ridge to collect money.

He said, 'If this has come from Brown, there is a good reason for them saying it, but you are wasting your time.'

Later he said, 'I have heard rumours for some time that efforts will be made if possible to shift the blame.'

Ridge, when seen, said he had been to the club casually. He absolutely denied receiving any money for any purpose at any time or authorising or instructing anyone to receive it for him.

Sir Harry said that in 1956 Brown changed his name by deed poll to Bennett and went into the metal business in London. Between April 29th and May 4th he went to Belgium. In June he went to Brighton to collect a cheque from a shop, and as he was leaving he was hailed by Heath, who told him that he must be doing well with his Rolls-Royce. Brown replied that he was 'getting by'. Heath 'then began the line that seemed to be common around here,' by saying, 'More than I am doing – things are very bad.'

Heath told him that there were inquiries for him at Bournemouth for a 'screwing job' at a jewellers which involved thousands of pounds. Brown told him he must be mad and that it was nothing to do with him, but he wanted the matter settled.

He went on to explain his movements, and Heath asked him to be at Brighton police station at six o'clock that night. Brown said he would come round, and he gave Heath £10.

Day Two

On Tuesday, the second day of the trial, there were the usual groups of people outside, anxious to catch a glimpse of the defendants. The weather being cold and overcast, most people were wearing thick coats with the collars turned up. Some had been queuing for hours.

As the court went into session Gerald Howard QC stood up and addressed the magistrates.

'Before I call any witnesses,' he said to a court suddenly hushed, 'there is a matter I should mention to you. You will recollect the very proper warning you gave about any possible interfering with witnesses. I have been instructed that such attempts have been made. I thought it fair to mention it now, in case the bench thought fit to reinforce their warning.'

The chairman, Howard Vokins, said, 'This is a very serious matter. A warning was given by a colleague of mine that any interference with witnesses would be dealt with very seriously indeed.'

Mr. Howard, returning to his feet, replied, 'I will have further details later in the day, when I might raise the matter again.'

The day's first witness (a smart, well-dressed man in a dark suit, with a white handkerchief showing in his top pocket and giving an address in Mayfair, London) arrived in a Rolls-Royce. Alan Bennett, his hair smartly groomed, a gold watch chain showing across his waistcoat, looked quite at ease.

When he began his evidence the court was informed that the five defendants were having difficulty in hearing him. Mr. Vokins agreed that the acoustics were bad, and he allowed the

The dapper Alan Bennett, formerly known as Brown, gave police officers money at his club. [Author's collection]

defendants to leave the dock and sit in the well of the court. Bennett then left the box and went to the opposite side of the court to continue his evidence.

He told the court that he changed his name by deed poll. He had been known as Alan Roy Brown and was also known as Ferguson. He had not been in any trouble since 1949. He bought the Astor Hotel in Kings Road in the autumn of 1954 and lived there with his wife, Wenche (pronounced Winkie). He converted part of the hotel into a club, calling it the Astor Club. At this time he did not know Tony Lyons.

'He came to the club a few days after opening. He asked me how I was going to run it. I told him that I wanted to run it in order to make money. I was given to understand that if I was not greedy, I could run it as I wanted. At that time I had never seen Ridge but he came into the club once with Tony Lyons and on a few occasions on his own.

'Later he came in with Lyons, and on that occasion he had a chat with Lyons about money, out of earshot of Ridge. The sum mentioned was a "score", meaning £20. The payment would be once a week, and I understood it would go to Ridge. When they left I went to the front door with them and outside I had a mark VII Jaguar. It was parked outside the entrance to the hotel. Ridge said, "That's a nice motor car. I can't afford one like that. I don't know how you do it." Ridge added, "My wife likes nice things." '

Bennett had said, 'So does mine. Don't worry: it will be taken care of.'

Lyons had come to the club quite often, bringing other customers, usually at about 11.30 pm to midnight: the proper closing time was 10.30 pm.

'If they had money then they had drinks.'

Mr. Howard said, 'Did Ridge go to the club again after the time he was there with Lyons?'

'Yes, he came once a week for his money. I gave him the money – four £5 notes a week. He came about five o'clock in the evening when nobody was in the club.'

Mr. Howard: 'When did you open the club?'

'It was no use opening before 10.30 pm in the evening. That was the time we started taking money. There were a few people in before that time. I gave money to Ridge six or seven times. The last time I gave him any money was before he went on his holidays to Spain. I gave it to him in Sherry's bar. Tony Lyons was the manager. Lyons was in the bar corner but I don't know whether he saw any money being handed over. I shouldn't think so – the money was wrapped in a newspaper.'

After Ridge went on his holidays, Heath came into the club.

'Heath said, "I want to speak to you privately," and we went into the lounge, as the secretary was at reception.'

Heath told him that from now on he (Heath) would be calling for the present.

'I said, "What present?". Heath said, "The present from the club." I said, "Has Ridge sent you?" He said, "Yes." I think it was then near the end of the week. I gave him the money. I think it was £20.'

Mr. Howard asked, 'Did you give money to Heath more than once?'

'Yes, it was many times.'

'How often did he come to the club?'

'Every week, sometimes twice.'

As he was giving evidence Bennett looked across at the five accused men, who were making notes.

Bennett said that the call was made same time each week, roughly between 5 and 6 in the evening. He said that he went away at the end of the season – about the beginning or middle of October – to the south of France. He closed the club and never reopened it.

'Heath called regularly once a week up to that time. Each time I saw him I gave him money. It was £20 for the weekly visits, and I also gave him some clothing.'

At this stage Mr. Howard produced four ties, which he said had been found in Heath's home. He handed these to Bennett who said, 'I gave three of these to Heath. I'm not sure about the fourth one, though.'

Bennett told the court that he had asked Heath if he got his share of the payments. Heath told him that it was a few pounds, nothing much. He was not always present when Heath called. If he was going to be away when Heath called he put four £5 notes in an envelope and left it in the bar. His wife served in the bar – occasionally a part time girl called Joyce and he. When Bennett closed the club his wife stayed to look after the hotel.

Mr. Howard then referred to a photograph of Bennett which the witness agreed as shown to him by Heath. Bennett said, 'He came to my office and asked if he could have a word with me in private. I took him to my private room. He put his hand in his pocket and pulled out a photograph, a police photograph. He said, "We're rather surprised." I said, "Who's we?", and he said, "The gov'nor and I." It was a photograph of 10 years or more ago. Having seen it, I said, "I haven't changed much." Heath continued, "We're surprised, we didn't expect this." He kept on about it. I told Heath I was then a business man, chairman of a few companies. I asked him what he wanted and was it blackmail? I asked him what he really wanted. He said "The gov'nor has sent me."

'I said, "This is blackmail. Go and tell your gov'nor to go and jump off Brighton pier, not another penny – and I have a good mind to write to the commissioner about it.'

Bennett reached over and gripped the edge of the witness box, and said in a slightly raised voice, 'That was the only time he did not have any money.'

Continuing his evidence, Bennett told the court about a man named Alan Walker, who he said came to stay at the Astor Hotel during Ascot week in 1955.

Mr. Howard said, 'Did you and your wife get to know him very well?'

'He got to know us very well.'

One evening his wife went out to dinner with Walker and arrived back home alone. Later Heath and two other police officers came to the hotel and Heath said he wanted to speak to Bennett privately. In the hotel lounge Heath said, 'We have arrested Alan. Your wife was with him.'

Bennett said he answered, 'What has my wife got to do with Alan being arrested?' Heath replied that Alan was wanted for larceny and that Bennett knew very well that for anybody associating with him the police officers could have made it difficult. Bennett had said, 'The girl has done nothing,' to which Heath replied, 'Anyway, we have let her go.'

Heath then said, 'Just give us our whack of the grand.'

Bennett told the court, 'I said, "What grand?" He said, "The grand Alan has lost out of his bedroom." He meant £1,000. I said, "Why ask me?" He said, "Because you had it." I said that it was impossible – I had been at Ascot all day.

'He kept on about his "whack" of the grand. He got no whack of the grand because there was no grand to whack out. He got £30 or £40 to keep the wife's name out of the papers and keep it quiet. It was also to keep the hotel's name out of the paper, and Heath said, "That will be taken care of, don't worry." '

Bennett said that later on an inspector from Lowestoft visited his hotel and looked around, and after he had gone, Heath came. He said, 'He doesn't believe you haven't had it, neither do I.' Heath was referring to the inspector when he said 'he.' Bennett said that Heath once more asked for his whack.

'I said that he could not have a whack of nothing.'

Some time later Heath came to the hotel again and asked to see Bennett privately. He said that there was an enquiry in Leeds in connection with false cheques and Bennett said he had not been to Leeds for twenty years. Heath said, 'Well you will have to go, you know.'

Bennett had replied that this was ridiculous because he had done nothing, but Heath insisted that he would have to go.

'I gave him some money and it then appeared that I didn't have to go to Leeds. It was £15 or £20. It was so he would write to Leeds or do whatever he had to do, so that I didn't have to go to Leeds. I have never heard anything more about Leeds.'

Towards the end of the season Heath told him that he wanted to buy a motor car, that he had a little money, and that if he could find the deposit he could have the rest on hire purchase.

'I said to him, "Find the remainder of the hire purchase money."

Brighton Conspiracy Case

HUNDREDS OF POUNDS IN BRIBES, SAYS CROWN

◆

Club Owner's £20 a Week: Agreement With 'Fence': Offer to Conceal Record

DAILY TELEGRAPH REPORTER

Three Brighton detectives were paid hundreds of pounds over a period of nine years by people involved in police inquiries, it was said at Brighton yesterday, when the town's suspended chief constable, CHARLES RIDGE, two of his detectives and two other men were accused of conspiracy.

Sir HARRY HYLTON-FOSTER, Q.C., the Solicitor-General, made an opening speech lasting more than two and a half hours. He said that Ridge was paid £20 a week by a club owner.

He said that the two detectives, Insp. JOHN HAMMERSLEY and Sgt. TREVOR HEATH concluded a "gentlemen's agreement" with a Brighton "fence" under which they received payments in cash or goods in the shape of stolen property.

The three police officers are jointly charged with ANTHONY LYONS, 59, licensee, of Marine Gate, Brighton, and SAMUEL BELLSON, 42, bookmaker, of The Drive, Hove.

Four hours before the hearing began a queue formed for the few public seats available. To prevent

people and much of it must necessarily come from people generally described as shady sources. And, therefore, I submit it would be most unwise for anyone to form any conclusion about this case until the matter has been fully tried out."

WRIT SERVED

Former Policeman

Sir Harry told the magistrates that an incident involved Hammersley and Bellson and a former police officer named Barnard who was invalided out of the force in 1952 and became an inquiry agent. In the course of this work Barnard had to serve writs and in August, 1953, he had one to serve on Bellson.

A cutting from the Daily Telegraph during the Brighton conspiracy trial.

He said it was difficult to find money. I asked him how much the car was and he said £300 or something like that. The deposit was £120. He had the car outside on trial.'

Heath showed him a diamond ring which he had valued at £70. Bennett said that he did not want the ring but after a lot of talk he took it and gave Heath £70.

'I first asked him if it was his own property.'

Bennett said he had moved to his present address in Green Street this year, and since about the beginning of the year had an interest in a business in Albermarie Street. He went abroad on business 'nearly every week'. He told of a visit to Brighton to collect a cheque from a man called Myers. While he was collecting it his wife was in the car outside.'

At this time Bennett asked for a glass of water, which was brought by a court official.

Continuing his story he said that when he was getting back into his car he heard a voice shouting, 'Alan!' – and saw Heath. They shook hands.

'I was just about to get into my car again when Heath said, "Just a moment." I said, "What is it?" Heath said, "There's an inquiry out for you." I asked him where from, and he replied, "Bournemouth." I asked what was it about and he said, "They say you took £6,000 of jewellery from a shop." I asked him the date and he said that it was 30th April.'

'Where were you on that day?' Mr Howard asked.

Bennett replied, 'I was in Brussels.' He produced his passport from his pocket and threw it onto the clerk's table.

Mr Howard remarked, 'It's not necessary.'

Bennett retorted, 'It was necessary a few weeks ago.'

Continuing his evidence, he said Heath had said to him, 'You look to be doing all right – a big Rolls-Royce.'

'I told him that I was getting by. Heath said that the enquiry from Bournemouth was nothing to do with us, but I said that I wanted the matter cleared up. He told me to be at the police station at 6 pm and he would phone through.'

Mr. Howard asked, 'Were you worried about this Bournemouth affair?'

'I have never been worried about anything,' Bennett replied. 'All I have ever worried about was having my name plastered all over the newspapers and slandered by the police. I had nothing to do with Bournemouth. I gave him more money that same day. I paid to keep my name out of the newspapers. I was being blackmailed by the police.'

Bennett said that he gave Heath £10 that day. After visiting a restaurant he decided to go to the police station without waiting for 6 pm.

As Bennett continued his evidence Ridge made notes in a red-backed exercise book and the other two police officers wrote copiously in ledger-type books.

Bennett said that he left his wife in the car when he went to the CID office, where Heath took him into Hamersley's room.

'I asked Hammersley what was this trouble in Bournemouth. Heath said, "He has a cake of notes in his back pocket." Hammersley said, "About the Bournemouth job, we will find out about it. It has nothing to do with us." '

Bennett said that he was asked where he was on April 30th and had said that he couldn't quite remember but thought he was abroad. In any case he knew nothing about it. Hammersley told Heath to go and find out about it, and when he left Bennett thought he was going to phone Bournemouth. When Heath came back he said, 'Everything's all right now.'

'I said, "Just like that?" and Heath said, "Yes, just like that." He then asked me what business I was in, and I told that I was in the metal business. There was some discussion about the business and Heath said that it must be a good business and he had friends in the metal business. They asked me where my office was and my home address. I did not want them to have my home address, so I gave them the address of a flat I had the lease of in Paddington.'

Bennett added, 'In case I forget to tell you, Heath then told me not to forget John. I screwed up a couple of fivers and threw them on the floor. Hammersley never asked for the money and just said, "Thank you, Alan." '

Bennett said that after he came back from Belgium and Holland he received a message and phoned Heath. He told him that there was a 'W' out for him from Folkestone. Bennett explained that the 'W' was a warrant. Heath asked him to meet him in Brighton and they agreed to meet at the Bodega restaurant in Ship Street.

'Earlier that day I went to Scotland Yard,' Bennett said, 'and saw some police officers. One of these was Powell of the Fraud Squad. The following day, June 27th, I phoned Heath who told me that he had waited quite a while for him. I said I was sorry but I could not make it. In the meantime I had found out that everything was all right about the Folkestone business. Scotland Yard had let me walk out.

'Heath asked who had said it was all right. Was it a "cozzor", meaning police? I told him that it was. Heath said, "Can you trust it, because it is different from what I hear. However, a half will put it right down here."

Bennett was asked who had said that, and he pointed across the court room at Heath, saying, 'Heath said it.' Asked what was a half, Bennett replied 'Half a ton – £50.'

At this point the chairman, Mr. Vokins, adjourned for lunch. By then Bennett had been giving evidence for two hours and twenty-five minutes.

More than 100 people were queuing outside the court for the afternoon's session. Many women were standing and knitting and a number of men were reading their newspapers, while others were talking among themselves, all anxious to get into the court.

Mr. John Bosley began cross examining Bennett on behalf of the chief constable, Charles Ridge.

'You know that Mr. Ridge denies your story?' he began.

Bennett replied, 'I would not expect him to admit it, sir.'

Mr. Bosley continued, 'You know he says he met you when you invited him to look at your club in the spring or summer of 1955?'

'Certainly, he met me.'

'It is a question of seeing who has to be believed, you or Mr. Ridge. Would you agree with me that it is right their worships should know a little more about your character?'

Bennett replied, 'My character is bad, I admit that, but let me tell you I have never resorted to blackmail, like your clients have.'

Mr. Bosley continued, 'Is it right you have used seven different names in your time?'

'That is lies. I have never used seven different names.'

He did admit to using the three already mentioned in court.

Mr Bosley then asked him about his previous convictions, and Bennett admitted to stealing, larceny servant, larceny from a dwelling, obtaining by false pretences, stealing by a trick, posing as an RAF pilot, being found in a dwelling house for unlawful purposes, receiving, housebreaking and larceny, shop-breaking and larceny on different occasions and unlawful wounding, although this offence was reduced to common assault.

'You say you have been of good behaviour for ten years? Many people say that. Do you say if the justices or another court have to decide between the word of yourself or Mr. Ridge you should be believed?'

'I say that Ridge is no better than me, but I have been convicted and he has not.'

Bennett had a habit of thumbing the ends of his moustache as he answered questions, although nothing was said about this. He was asked how he arrived at court this morning and Bennett stated that he arrived in his Rolls-Royce.

Mr Bosley continued his cross examination, gradually working through all aspects of Bennett's evidence.

Mr. Cyril Wheeler, for Heath, asked him about Walker.

'I didn't know that Walker had a record,' Bennett answered.

He said he knew nothing about the alleged theft of £1,000 from Walker. He went to Ascot on that day and only found out about it on his return.

'Walker gave me some money to take to Ascot to put bets on for him. It was £150 and he lost £120, and I returned the £30 to him.'

Mr. Wheeler continued, 'Did you find the running of this club a very profitable occupation?'

'I earned a living.'

'Was it a good, bad or indifferent living?'

'It was a living; a decent living.'

'At the end of the season you were able to go to the south of France?'

'I had gone to the south of France for many years.'

Mr David Peck, representing John Hammersley, stood up, asking the court's permission.

'When you came into court today,' he asked Bennett, 'did you say something to Hammersley?'

'I never spoke to Hammersley.'

'Did you say, "I think you are being framed?" '

Bennett replied, 'Are you having a joke? Certainly not.'

He was then asked about making statements to Scotland Yard officers.

'I made a longish statement to Superintendent Forbes-Leith,' Bennett said, 'and named certain people, but that was much later on.'

Mr Wheeler, continuing his cross-examination, asked, 'Was it right you were later arrested for the Folkestone affair?'

Bennett said, 'I was never arrested. I went in and gave myself up. I was tried and acquitted.'

Mr Wheeler continued, 'There was a genuine inquiry about you by Folkestone?'

Bennett replied, 'There was a genuine inquiry for a person, but not a Bennett.'

'When you were in Brighton on June 19th this year, driving your car, you stopped when you saw Heath.'

'My dear sir,' Bennett replied, 'Heath would be the last one I would stop my car and wave to. He stopped me. I do agree I got out and into his car and then got out again.'

'Is it right,' Mr Wheeler asked, 'that when you were interviewed by Hammersley and Heath you adopted a very indignant attitude over the Bournemouth affair?'

Bennett replied, 'I protested my innocence.'

Mr. Wheeler continued to cross-examine for a short while longer, indicating to the bench that he had just a little further to go.

'Did you threaten you would complain to the home office about being accused over the Bournemouth affair?' he asked.

'No, but years ago I threatened I would report a matter to a former home secretary I knew, which I should have done. That was years ago.'

'Did you threaten at any other time you would complain to the home office?'

'In the summer of 1955 over one of Heath's blackmailing incidents, namely the photograph.'

'Why did you pay the money if you had nothing to fear?'

'I wanted my past to be forgotten. I wanted to be just left alone.

By going to Scotland Yard everybody in the world knows about this, and it has stopped me getting a living.'

'You were willing to pay, although you had nothing to fear, because of your past?'

'That is the only answer there can be.'

The magistrates now adjourned the hearing until the following day. Bennett's evidence had taken three hours and 12 minutes, and for 45 minutes of that time he had been cross-examined.

Day Three

As the time for the court hearing approached a queue of some 70 people had formed, most of them men, anxious to get into the public gallery to listen to the witnesses and to see the defendants.

With the magistrates in place, the first witness arrived. She was a white-haired woman dressed entirely in black and wearing a feathered hat. She entered the witness box and told of a visit she made to the police station at the town hall.

She was Mrs Blanche Josephine Cherryman, and she lived at the Royal Hotel in King's Road. It used to be called the Astor Hotel but

had changed its name. She said the Astor Club closed at different times, but never before 1.30am. Everyone spoke about it as being a 'bad' club, and she knew that to be right. There were always lots of fights, drunkenness and trouble with women there.

She said, 'I went to Brighton police station on 4th October, 1955, to report what was going on at the club. I went again later and asked to see Mr. Ridge alone. I didn't know who to trust in the CID.'

Mr. Maxwell Turner, prosecuting, said, 'What did you tell Ridge about the Astor Club?'

Mrs Blanche Cherryman.
[Author's collection]

'I cannot tell you exactly,' she replied, 'but I told him what was going on at the Astor Club, how it was being run, how late it was and the drunkenness that was going on there.'

Before that visit she had taken a telephone call one night. The speaker had said, 'Close the club tonight,' adding that she was to say it was Charlie speaking.

'When you told Ridge what was going on at the Astor Club,' Mr Turner asked, 'did he make any comment?'

She replied that as far as she could remember he said he would see into it.

Answering a question from Mr. John Bosley for Ridge, Mrs Cherryman said she might have told Ridge that Bennett owed her £2,000. She told Mr. Cyril Wheeler, for Heath, that when Bennett closed the club he still owed her £2,000 – and, indeed, it had not yet been repaid.

That ended Mrs Cherryman's evidence. Mrs Bennett then returned to the witness box: she had been late in arriving at court that morning. She was quizzed by Mr Stanley Rees QC, representing Anthony Lyons.

14 *Daily Telegraph and Morning Post, Tuesday, November 26, 1931*

Brighton Conspiracy Case

HUNDREDS OF POUNDS IN BRIBES, SAYS CROWN

Club Owner's £20 a Week: Agreement With 'Fence': Offer to Conceal Record

DAILY TELEGRAPH REPORTER

Three Brighton detectives were paid hundreds of pounds over a period of nine years by people involved in police inquiries, it was said at Brighton yesterday, when the town's suspended chief constable, CHARLES RIDGE, two of his detectives and two other men were accused of conspiracy.

Sir HARRY HYLTON-FOSTER, Q.C., the Solicitor-General, made an opening speech lasting more than two and a half hours. He said that Ridge was paid £20 a week by a club owner.

He said that the two detectives, Insp. JOHN HAMMERSLEY and Sgt. TREVOR HEATH concluded a "gentlemen's agreement" with a Brighton "fence" under which they received payments in cash or goods in the shape of stolen property.

The three police officers are jointly charged with ANTHONY LYONS, 59, licensee, of Marine Gate, Brighton, and SAMUEL BELLSON, 42, bookmaker, of The Drive, Hove.

Four hours before the hearing began a queue formed for the few public seats available. To prevent

people and much of it must necessarily come from people generally described as shady sources. And, therefore, I submit it would be most unwise for anyone to form any conclusion about this case until the matter has been fully tried out."

WRIT SERVED

Former Policeman

Sir Harry told the magistrates that an incident involved Hammersley and Bellson and a former police officer named Barnard who was invalided out of the force in 1952 and became an inquiry agent. In the course of this work Barnard had to serve writs and in August, 1953, he had one to

Another cutting from the Daily Telegraph. The case filled column after column for a full two weeks. [Author's collection]

42

'Did criminals go to the club?' he asked her.

She replied, 'I have seen some criminals there.'

'The Astor Club – was it known as the Bucket of Blood?'

She nodded.

She was in the witness box for a little under two hours, including an hour the previous day. During that time she answered more questions from Mr. Maxwell Turner about some messages she had handed to her husband on his return from abroad. He asked her for her telephone number, and she asked nervously, 'May I not give it, because I have had so many reporters.'

She was allowed to write her telephone number down on a piece of paper and hand it to the magistrates. Mr. Turner then said, 'There is a question I should have asked you earlier. Was the Astor Club ever raided by the police while your husband and you were there?'

'Never, no,' she replied.

Mr. Bosley, representing Ridge, then asked a number of personal questions, such as when she and Bennett were married, and about her nationality.

'Have you talked over your evidence with your husband,' he asked. 'I mean after he gave his evidence and before you started yours?'

'There isn't much to talk about,' she replied.

'You lunched with your husband yesterday during his evidence, didn't you?'

'I did, and there was present also a police superintendent. He wouldn't let us talk about the case at all.'

While his wife was giving her evidence, Mr. Bennett was sitting on the opposite side of the court listening intently. He was, as usual, immaculately dressed. He wore a silver-grey suit with an inch or two of white shirt cuff showing and gold cuff links protruding discreetly from his sleeve. He smiled occasionally when she answered her questions. At the end of her evidence she walked across the court and joined him at the back.

The ninth witness to give evidence was Mrs. Mary Mason of Montpelier Road. She was wearing a black coat and yellow hat and sat in the witness box while giving her evidence.

In answer to Mr. Gerald Howard, she said she reopened the Astor Club in January 1956. She said that she knew Tony Lyons and he had told her how the club was run in Brown's time. He said that Alan Brown used to pay money to do as he liked.

'He said something to the effect of £20 a week – not to police officers mind you, but to Mr. Lyons, and that he spent half the money back again. It was a business arrangement. By that I understood Mr. Lyons had had an interest in the club – to bring people there.'

Mrs. Mason was asked by Mr. Howard if she knew whether the Astor Club closed down at any time while Brown was running it.

'I didn't know it, I heard it,' she said. 'Tony Lyons more or less gave me to understand that Brown knew somebody who told him when the place was likely to be raided by the police and he closed down for a few days. He asked me how I was getting along with the club and I said I was getting by, I was getting a living. From his manner I thought he would have liked me to have the same arrangement as Brown had. It was never said to me openly.'

'Were you ever raided by the police?'

'No.'

'Did you ever pay any money to anybody?'

'Never.'

The magistrates then called for an interval for lunchtime, and the court broke up. A larger crowd than usual waited through the lunch break to see the comings and goings of witnesses and other leading people in the case.

The court re-convened at 2 o'clock, and the first witness was Mrs. Margaret Newman, an auburn haired woman dressed in a fur coat and black hat. She gave her address as Almorah Road, Islington, London, and the daughter of Mrs. Mason, the previous witness.

She told how she helped by serving behind the bar in her mother's club. Tony Lyons, who she knew, came to the club usually with friends. He was a member.

'When he came in with friends,' Mr Howard asked, 'did these friends sign the visitors' book?'

'At times.'

She said that on one occasion she handed him the visitors' book and he told her it wasn't necessary.

'I didn't know who were members and who were not, and as Mr. Lyons had been there a long time before I went there I took his word for it.'

She spoke of often going to Sherry's bar and being there after the Astor Club was raided. She said, 'My mother's club being raided was a topic of conversation. My mother thought she had been victimised. Mr. Lyons said that it was very unfair, and my mother also said it was unfair.'

Mrs Newman said that people were talking about how the club was run in Brown's day.

The tenth witness was Harry Waterman of Beresford Road, London, who said that he knew Bennett. In 1955 he went to the Astor Club before the club was open and then when the club did open he helped at times.

'I did no particular job,' he said. 'I wasn't paid for it. I helped generally for a friend of mine. I was helping more or less until Mr. Bennett left the club.'

Mr. Waterman said that on one occasion he saw Bennett at the club put some money in a newspaper, and later, at Sherry's bar in Brighton, saw Bennett hand a newspaper to someone. He said that he couldn't be absolutely certain about identifying the person to whom the newspaper was handed, but asked if he could see anyone who resembled that person in court, he pointed straight to Ridge.

He said that Heath came to the Astor Hotel while he was there, and that he once saw Bennett put some money in an envelope and hand it to Heath. Mr. Waterman added that a number of years ago he was convicted of receiving and bound over, and that he also had another conviction for receiving for which he received 12 months imprisonment.

The next witness was Detective Sergeant Arthur Broadbent-Speight, of Leeds City Police.

In 1955, he told the hearing, Leeds City Police were investigating an offence of obtaining property in Leeds on a cheque which was subsequently dishonoured. They wished Brighton Police to interview a man called Austin Ferguson, alias Brown. On August 23rd 1955 they wrote to Brighton Police in connection with this.

Asked if, as a result of this letter they ever succeeded in having an interview with Ferguson, Sergeant Speight said, 'No.'

'Did you know that Ferguson had a total of seven different names?' asked Mr Bosley.

'Not to my knowledge,' Speight replied. 'Only four – Ferguson, Wood, Brown and Bennett.'

'Holt, Montgomery and Poyner?', Mr Bosley added.

Mr. Maxwell-Turner, re-examining, asked if the Leeds City Police wanted Ferguson to go to Leeds. Sergeant Speight replied, 'No, sir.'

The next witness was Detective Sergeant George Dunstan of Brighton Borough Police. He was handed the force's official message book and asked to look at message no. 1,043.

Sergeant Dunstan said that it was written in his handwriting and dated May 1st 1957.

Mr. Maxwell-Turner: 'Did Brighton Police have an inquiry from Bournemouth Police about an offence of shop-breaking at Bournemouth?'

'Yes.'

Sergeant Dunstan was the last witness of the day, and the court was adjourned until the morning.

The Don

In the 1940s and 50s there were several gangs in London, all vying for 'a piece of the action' and all trying to make huge profits from their illegal activities. Some of them, such as the Krays and the Richardsons, were to become household names. Perhaps the best known gangland character in the early days was 'Jack Spot' (real name Jack Comer), a Jewish criminal who controlled much of the East End of London during the 1930s, 40s and 50s.

By the 1950s,however, there was a new 'top dog' – the so-called Soho Don. His real name was Billy Howard. His word was law and his brutal associates saw to it that it remained so . . .

Three days after the start of the Brighton hearing, Betty Lawrence received a visit. It was almost midnight on a cold wintry evening. She was walking in the town centre, wearing an astrakhan coat with the fur collar pulled up high around her face against the chill.

She hadn't taken much notice of the dark coloured car that cruised slowly past her and then turned the street corner and came to a stop. Four men dressed in expensive dark suits got out of the car, their scarred faces indicating that they were tough guys and had been involved in many gangland scraps. They certainly weren't the sort of people law abiding citizens would care to have as friends.

As she reached the corner of the street one of the men grabbed her by the shoulder and pushed her, almost casually, into the arms of one of the others. Gently he pushed her back again. By this time the men had formed a circle and Betty was piggy-in-the-middle.

She cried out in a faltering and frightened voice, 'What do you want?'

One of the men answered in a sneering and menacing way, 'We're Billy Howard's boys, see and we got a message for ya.'

Her fear was etched on her face.

'I don't know Billy Howard.'

'I know, love,' said one of the men, who appeared to be the leader, 'but he knows you.'

He gave her a shove, this time a lot harder than before.

'He told us to tell you that you're not to say anything against our friends in court.'

His voice trembled as he spoke, and he then took a razor from his pocket, opened it and put the cold, flat side to her face. He gently pressed it and it made a small cut in her skin – harder, and it would have sliced her face.

Another of the men said, 'You'd better do as he says 'cos if you don't Billy Howard's going to come down here himself, and he'll cut ya tongue out and then chop you into little bits.'

One of them chuckled as he pushed Betty again across the circle. This time no one caught her and she fell against the wall, stumbling and twisting her ankle. She was visibly shaken and very scared, because although she didn't know Billy Howard it was obvious he was a big London gang leader. And he knew about her.

The men walked calmly back to their car, glancing back as they got into it, and sped off northwards.

It was this story that Gerald Howard QC would report to a hushed court in the Brighton Police trial the following day.

A few days later Michael Pilley, a reporter for the *Daily Sketch* who knew Billy Howard, was interviewing him in the club he frequented. Pilley came straight out with the question people wanted to hear answered.

'Did you send your boys down to Brighton to threaten Mrs. Betty Lawrence at midnight two days ago,' he asked, 'and have them tell her that she would be sliced up if she gave evidence?'

Howard continued to sip his triple gin and tonic, glanced up at the ceiling and after a while said with a slight smile, 'I don't have any boys.'

Pilley looked around and focussed his gaze on a group of burly men a few feet from where they were sitting.

'Well, apart from these boys,' Howard said with a slowly spreading grin.

Pilley took another swig at his drink, supplied by Howard, and said, 'So you're not the West End Chopper Man, then?'

Howard paused a while before saying, 'I think it's a bleeding cheek – a liberty.'

'There's a special watch for you on roads into Brighton and at the railway station,' Pilley said.

One of the burly men sitting close by threw in, 'I've only got three months to live, but I'll say this before I go – Billy's a gentleman.'

Just then Michael Brown, another crime reporter, appeared in the club and showed Howard the headlines in the latest edition of a newspaper. The front page linked Howard's name with the Brighton case. It accused him of attempting to pervert the course of justice by using threats of violence, namely a slash from an open razor, against witnesses who had said they were prepared to give evidence.

Howard slowly read the headlines, and said in a quiet voice, 'I am a peaceful man, I didn't threaten anyone. I live for my wife and children. No one from Scotland Yard has been to see me. They know where I am and my conscience is clear.'

He said this in a kind of a statement, but with some sort of sincerity. And it was true enough that the police knew where to find Billy Howard, as did the many newspaper reporters and half of London's night club and casino managers.

The following day, predictably, Billy Howard and Michael Pilley made the headlines as was predicted. The solicitor acting for Howard wasted no time in speaking to the editor of the *Daily Sketch*. The following day the newspaper carried this retraction:

THE SPANISH GARDEN CLUB

It has been suggested to us that an article in yesterday's Daily Sketch has been read as meaning that the Spanish Garden Club, Mayfair, is owned by Billy Howard, to whom reference was made in proceedings at Brighton. Mr. Howard is not the proprietor of the club, although he is a member of it.

The lease on the property and the licence were held by Peggy, a girlfriend of Howard's. There was nothing on paper that could connect him to the club.

At this time Howard was 40 years old and had a string of convictions that had begun during his teenage years and had resulted in spells in borstal, together with a number of convictions for illegal gambling which, although not custodial, would have prevented him from holding a liquor licence. Any acknowledgement that Howard had financial or operational control of the Spanish Garden Club could have caused the closure of what was a lucrative business.

Day Four

On the morning the usual crowds gathered around the town hall area, anxious to see anyone who was involved in the case. By the time the doors were opened, a queue of more than 60 people was waiting. People filed in, quiet but excited, hoping to hear something sensational.

Before the proceedings opened, Gerald Howard QC rose and, looking very serious, asked to address the bench. The movements being made by people wandering into court, the adjusting of chairs, dulled chatter from those in the public gallery – all suddenly ceased. It was obvious by his demeanour that something sensational was about to happen.

Addressing Mr. Vokins he spoke slowly and deliberately, picking his words with care.

'Last night in the town centre,' he began, 'a woman witness for the prosecution, Mrs. Elizabeth Lawrence, who is yet to give evidence in this case, was threatened by persons who said that they were Billy Howard's boys.'

Mr Howard stopped and glanced around, first to the left and then to the right, waiting for the court to digest his words. He then said that Mrs Lawrence had been told that she would be cut with a razor if she went ahead and gave evidence to the court. People in all parts of the room looked at the defendants, but they gave no sign of knowing anything about the incident.

Mr Vokins, looking angry, reiterated his words from the early part of the trial about witnesses being interfered with. Mr. Howard apologised to the court for having to report the matter, but said that he had no option but to bring it to the knowledge of the magistrates.

The day's first witness was John Stopler. Rather than mention where he lived, where he worked and his telephone number, he wrote the details down and handed them to the magistrates. The clerk was instructed to include the details with the depositions. Mr. Stopler was the 18th witness of the hearing. He said that Alan Bennett had the tenancy of an office in his suite and on 25th June this year there had been a telephone message for Bennett. He took the message, which said that Mr. Bennett was wanted urgently at Brighton. Would he come and see Mr Trevor Heath or Mr. Hammersley? He must not come by car.

Stopler, a tall, dark-haired bespectacled man dressed in a smart clerical suit, said that he wrote this message down and later telephoned it to Bennett's private address, where Bennett's wife answered the telephone.

The following witness was Det Sgt Frederick Powell of Scotland Yard. He said that on June 26th a man named Bennett had called at Scotland Yard at around 5 pm. He had not been asked to come there, but came on his own accord. At the time Powell knew nothing about either Bennett or the breaking and entering at Folkestone.

Gerald Howard QC, for the Crown, advised the magistrates that the next six or seven witnesses were all employees of various post office telephone exchanges who would formally prove a number of telephone calls. Three of them were telephonists from Brighton telephone exchange in North Road.

One of them produced a record of a call made from Brighton 25899 to a number which was written down on a small piece of paper, shown to her and then handed to the magistrates. Then a man and three women telephonists from the London Faraday exchange gave evidence. Three of them said that they had connected calls from a number – written on a slip of paper and shown to them – to Brighton 24141.

With this evidence completed, the telephonists were released from the court. However two of them chose to sit at the back of the court, where they listened intently.

The next witness was Mrs. Alice Brabiner. She was dressed in a brown coat and was hatless. She sat alongside a Brighton police-woman sergeant. Two women prison officers stood close by.

Mr. Howard said to her, 'I can see that you are upset, but please try and answer my questions.

'You are at present serving a sentence of imprisonment for procuring an abortion.'

Mrs. Brabinger answered in a quiet voice, which was hardly audible: 'Yes.'

Several times throughout her evidence she was asked to speak a little louder. She told the hushed court that she had been living in a basement flat in Regency Square in Brighton. Her daughter, Mrs. Iris Karrouze, was living there with her. On November 26th the previous year she had met Betty Lawrence and as a result of a conversation she went to Vernon Terrace, Brighton.

Mr. Howard said, 'I know this is painful for you, but do tell us who was in the flat.'

Mrs. Brabinger said, 'A girl, Betty Lawrence and I, and I saw some children on the stairs.'

'Did you do anything in the flat on this occasion?'

'Yes, sir.'

'You have told us you are serving your sentence for procuring an abortion. Did you perform some sort of operation on this girl?'

'Yes, sir.'

'With what sort of instrument?'

'A syringe, which belonged to Betty Lawrence.'

She said that she knew Detective Sergeant Heath, who came to her house on Christmas Eve. He was with another man and he told her he knew that she had been to Vernon Terrace, Brighton.

'I denied I had been there,' she continued, 'and made a statement to him.'

Early in the new year Heath went to her flat again with another detective at about 8 pm, and soon afterwards the other detective left. Sergeant Heath asked her daughter to go into the kitchen and make him some tea.

'He then said to me if I paid him some money he might be able to help me. I asked him in which way he could help. He said that if I paid him money, it would go a long way. He said that even if I won the football pools it would not keep me out of trouble I was in, but he would help me if I gave him money.'

She said that she didn't know whether Betty Lawrence was a member of the Celebrity Club, but about a week after Heath visited her she went to the club and saw her there. She said that she had a conversation with her, and soon after that her daughter, Iris, left the club.

'I sent her home. When she came back she gave me £25 in £1 notes. It was in an envelope, and I gave it to Betty Lawrence who went out of the club. I stayed in the club. She telephoned me later and then my daughter came back into the club again. After a conversation with her she went out and came back with the £25 in the envelope.

'I telephoned Mr. Heath at the town hall. I said to him, "What's it all about?" He asked me where I was. He told me to stay there as it was raining hard and he would be there in ten minutes. He said he would bring his car and stop at the bottom of the steps – that way we wouldn't get wet. I went out and got into his car. He asked me if Maxi was in the club.'

Mrs. Brabinger said 'Maxi' was Mr. Betts. He was in the club but she told Heath he had gone. Heath told her that he didn't want Maxi to know about the money. He asked her if she had the money, and she then gave it to Heath.

Heath told her that Betty Lawrence had asked him to tear the statement up, but he couldn't do that.

'I saw Heath again two or three times a week at my flat after this meeting.'

Mr. Howard asked, 'Had you ever heard about 'corrective training?'

She replied that she had now, but not at that time.

'When did you find out about it?'

'I found out when I was in prison.'

'When Heath came to see you did you see any papers – documents of any sort?'

'No.'

'Did you give him any more money?'

'Yes.'

'Can you remember how much more you gave him?'

'I think it was £15, not to bring me corrective training papers.'

'Had you any sort of idea of the sentence you were likely to get?'

'He told me I could get 14 years.'

'Who told you that?'

'Mr. Heath.'

Mr. Howard continued, 'You have just told the court you gave him £15 not to bring corrective training papers. Did you give him any more?'

'Yes, I gave him various sums of money until the day I was tried.'

'Approximately how much in all did you give him?'

'£68.'

Mrs. Brabinger said that the day before she went to trial she met Heath in Regency Square as he was on his way to her flat, and she gave him £8.

'Did you say anything to him?'

'Yes sir, I asked him if he could wait until after the trial.'

'Wait for what, Mrs. Brabinger?'

At this point she broke down and sobbed. The policewoman sergeant put her arm around her, and a court official brought her a glass of water. After taking a few sips she answered, 'Heath said, you don't back a horse after the race.'

Mr. Howard allowed a few minutes to pass before he asked her if she felt able to carry on. She nodded that she was.

'On the day before your trial, when you told the court you gave him £8, how much money had you got altogether?'

'Do you mean how much money I had left, sir?'

'No, how much did you possess on that day, when you parted with the £8?'

'I'm not sure sir, but it was between £11 and £15.'

'What were you going to do with that money?'

'I had intended leaving it to my daughter because she had been out of work looking after me.'

'This is my last question to you Mrs. Brabinger,' he said. 'How long a sentence did you receive?'

'Fifteen months,' she replied.

David Peck, representing John Hammersley, asked her whether Hammersley was one of the two officers that she referred to in her evidence. She replied that she knew Mr. Hammersley, and that it wasn't him on either occasion.

Answering Cyril Wheeler, who represented Trevor Heath, she agreed that she had three convictions altogether: in 1941 for larceny (theft), when she was fined; in 1949 for abortion, when she was given a conditional discharge for 12 months; and in April that year when she was convicted for abortion, for which she was now serving a prison sentence.

She was asked whether Heath had called at her home on some occasions to get particulars of her antecedents and history.

'No,' she said. 'He didn't want particulars, all he wanted was tea.'

She agreed that on one occasion he served her with a notice relating to her appearance, but said he did not serve her with a notice of corrective training. Replying to another question, she said that she had two daughters living in Canada, and she had told Heath that she had thought of going there. She was asked if she had shown Heath photographs of her daughters.

'Yes, he made me very angry. He said he wanted to see if any of my daughters had ever been in trouble.'

Mr Wheeler then asked if she knew that the prosecution case was that the first suggestion of money came from her.

She replied, 'I did offer him money.'

'You did not say that this morning?'

'I wasn't asked,' she replied. 'I said it in my statement to the police.'

During a short re-examination by Mr. Maxwell Turner, another Crown counsel, Mrs. Brabinger said that she offered Heath some money on Christmas Eve. Asked what she said to him, she replied, 'I said, "Can't you take a few pounds and forget about it?" '

Asked if she knew before her last conviction whether or not she was eligible for corrective training, she replied, 'No, I didn't know anything about it.'

This completed Mrs. Brabinger's evidence. She had spent a total of one hour in the witness box.

The next witness was Reginald Betts. He told the magistrates that he was on the stage from time to time under the name of Max Ray.

'I have known Mrs. Brabinger between 11 and 12 years,' he said.

Last Christmas Eve he was at her flat when Heath and another man called and went into the kitchen with Mrs. Brabinger. They were there for about half an hour. After Heath and the other man had left, Mrs. Brabinger came back rather white and shaken.

'I was at the flat on another occasion when Sergeant Heath called and saw Mrs. Brabinger in the kitchen,' he continued. 'After he left she seemed rather worried and shaken. She was rather ill. She had been, apparently, since the first night on Christmas Eve.'

Betts continued that in the Celebrity Club Mrs. Brabinger showed him an envelope containing a number of £5 notes. He stated that he saw her leave the club and get into Heath's car, where she remained for about ten minutes or maybe a quarter of an hour.

Betts completed his evidence and the magistrates adjourned for lunch. The magistrates had now heard from 28 of the 60 or so witnesses.

Throughout the morning session there were people queuing outside, and by the time the afternoon session was about to begin the crowd had grown considerably outside the main doors. The police brought in extra officers to control the crowd. They were forced to push people away from the doors and let them enter in relays. When all the seats inside the courtroom were full, the doors were shut, leaving around a hundred people outside.

The first witness in the afternoon was Mrs. Iris Karrouze, who said she was the daughter of Mrs. Brabinger and now lived in Ventnor Villas, Hove. Until the time her mother went to prison they had lived together in Regency Square. She said that she first met Trevor Heath just after last Christmas.

Mr. Maxwell Turner asked, 'How many times can you remember Sergeant Heath coming to your flat?'

'He almost lived with us,' she said. 'He was always down there. If it wasn't the morning then it was the afternoon.

'On one occasion, after Heath had been alone with my mother for about ten minutes, she fainted, and quite often after seeing Heath her nerves were bad.'

The next and 30th witness was Mrs. Gladys Elizabeth (Betty) Lawrence of Vernon Terrace, Brighton. She was wearing a dark grey coat and a black hat, and looking very smart. On a request to the magistrates she was allowed to sit down in the witness box while she gave her evidence.

She said, 'I have known Mrs. Brabinger for about 18 months and before that I had known her by sight.'

The illegal operation for which Mrs. Brabinger was now serving a prison sentence took place at the flat where Mrs. Lawrence was living. She had introduced to Mrs. Brabinger the girl on whom the operation was performed, and she was present when the operation took place. Mr. Turner asked her if she knew Heath at that time.

'I had seen him for a few years. I knew who he was, but I had never had any conversation with him.'

She first spoke to him on Christmas Eve, 1956. Heath sent for her and she saw him at the CID office at the police station. He told her that he wanted to see her about an operation which had taken place in her flat. He said he knew who had done it, because the young woman concerned had told him. She said it was true and made a statement.

'The next time I spoke to him was the following Sunday morning – that would be 30th December – in a public house. Heath asked for the syringe.'

Mr. Turner said, 'Being Sunday, I suppose your husband was at home?'

'Yes, Sergeant Heath said he would get a warrant to search the flat for it, but I promised to take it down at 9 o'clock on the Monday morning, which I did.'

She was then asked if she wanted her husband to know.

'No sir. The next time I saw Heath to speak to was in Sherry's bar in West Street. Heath was talking to Lyons at the far end of the bar.'

'What was the far end of the bar known as?'

'It was called "Tattersalls", sir.'

Mr. Turner asked, with a slight grin on his face, 'Is that more select than the silver ring at the other end?'

She said that the other end was called the Free Course, because they drank beer and orange. She said that Heath walked out of the bar and nodded to her to follow him. She did so. There was another officer with Heath. He walked out and up West Street to a police box across the road and called her inside. At this time all three of them were in the police box. Heath took another statement, very similar to the previous one. It was written in a notebook and she couldn't remember if she signed it or not.

She was asked if she ever discussed with Heath the fact that she didn't want her husband to know that she was mixed up in an abortion. She had asked Heath whether if she was mixed up in a case her name would be in the papers.

'Did you want your name to be in the papers?'

'No.'

'Did Heath make any suggestion to you as to what you should do?'

'He said, why didn't I want my name in. I said I was afraid my husband and children would find out about it. He told me to go and see Mr. Lyons. She was asked if she understood how he could keep her name out of the papers.

'I didn't know exactly what he meant by that.'

She said that she had known Lyons for about eight years. Asked if she took Heath's advice, Mrs. Lawrence said, 'Yes, I went to Sherry's bar that same evening. Lyons was in the bar. I spoke to the manageress, Mrs. Tucker, who then called Mr. Lyons.

'He said to me "You are in a spot of bother, Betty," but he didn't mention what it was. I said, "Yes, I understand you can help me." He replied, "Yes, it will cost you a ton." She asked Lyons what a ton meant and he said £100.

'Is £100 a lot of money to you?' Mr Turner asked.

'It certainly is. I said I had not got that amount of money, but I might be able to borrow £50. He said that would not be any good.'

'Did he say why it would not be any good?'

'No, he just walked away and I didn't have any more conversation with him about this business.

Mrs. Lawrence said she had not got Heath's home telephone number at that time.

'When I phoned the CID office for Sergeant Heath, he came and met me and then gave me his home telephone number and told me not to phone him at the CID office. I next met him outside the

GPO in his car. First of all I told him I did not have the money Mr. Lyons had mentioned. He said that if I could get £50, that would suit him.'

'Suit who?'

'I presumed it was Sergeant Heath. I beg your pardon, he said suit *me*.'

Heath had asked her how she was going to get the money.

'I said I had a friend in London who would be down the following week, and he would probably lend me the money.'

At this point, after nearly an hour in the witness box, Mrs. Lawrence appeared to go pale. Mr. Turner asked her if she was feeling all right, and the police woman sergeant went to her. Mrs. Lawrence wiped her brow with her handkerchief and one court official brought her a glass of water while another brought her some smelling salts. Two of the magistrates left their seats and opened the doors nearest to them at the back of the court, while court officials opened two more.

The chairman asked her if she would like a five-minute adjournment to go for some fresh air. She thanked him, but said she was now ready to carry on.

On the completion of her evidence, and as the court was about to be adjourned for the day, the magistrates announced that if a *prima facie* case was established at the Brighton hearing, the ensuing trial would be held at the Old Bailey.

Day Five

Friday the 29th was a bleak, wet and cold day with moderate winds, but that didn't stop the crowds flocking to the town hall. Soon after 7 am the queue started to form in Bartholomews, the older women, armed as usual with their knitting, having scarves tied tightly around their necks in an effort to keep the cold at bay. The main doors were opened 25 minutes before the start of the court, with police allowing a few in at a time. This was expected to be a big day in the trial, as Ernie Waite would be giving evidence. Rumours had been circulating for some time as to his involvement with the three police officers now on trial.

Ernie Waite. [Gordon Dean]

The first witness to enter the court was Arthur Thorn, a short dark haired man dressed in a smart blue suit. He was allowed to write his address down on a piece of paper and it was then passed to the magistrates. He said that he had a conversation with Mrs. Lawrence – the previous day's final witness – and drew a cheque for £25, which he gave her. Later he gave her another £25. He said that he was in a public house in Lewes after Mrs. Brabinger had been sentenced, and he heard Heath say to Mrs. Lawrence something to the effect that 'the money had been worth it'.

Ernie Waite was the next witness – the 32nd of the hearing. A dark-haired, thickset man, he wore a vivid blue waistcoat under a smart grey suit with a maroon bow tie.

He told the magistrates that he had lived in Preston Road since 1950, that he was divorced and that he had been in the greengrocery, fruit and poultry business all his working life. About a year ago Mrs. Joan Watson had taken over a shop in New England Road as a greengrocer and poulterer, and he managed it.

Gerald Howard QC for the prosecution asked if he knew Ridge.

Waite said that he had known him since about 1950. He said that he also knew a man named Matheson who had a cat and dog meat shop at Marine Gardens, Brighton. Waite said that he used the shop.

'What for?'

'For illegal meat.'

'How often would you go to that shop?'

'Every day practically.'

'Did you ever see Mr. Ridge at that shop?'

'Yes, mostly on a Friday evening.'

'What did he come for?'

'He came for his cat and dog meat, and he had a joint of meat.'

'What sort of meat?'

'Whatever was on the menu.'

Whose meat was it?'

'Well, I bought it. It was my meat.'

As Waite was giving this evidence, Ridge was writing furiously in the exercise book he had been using throughout the week.

Innocent times: the young Ernie Waite (holding the football) with a Brighton boys' team in Preston Park in the 1920s. [Gordon Dean]

'You say you used this shop for illegal meat,' Mr Howard continued, 'so the joints were part of the illegal meat?'

'Yes.'

'Did he pay for the meat he had?'

'No, sir.'

Waite said that periodically officials of the ministry of food carried out inspections in Brighton.

'Did you know when any such inspection was going to be carried out?'

'Yes.'

'How did you know?''

'A message was passed to Matheson. When there was such a message we kept the place pretty clear of human consumption meat. If we couldn't get it clear in time then we would spray it with green dye.'

Mr. Howard explained that meat sprayed in that way could not be sold for human consumption.

'Do you know John Hammersley?' he asked.

'I have known him for about eight years,' Waite replied. 'He has been to all my shops.'

'What did he come for?'

'Dog meat, joints and chicken occasionally.'

'Were those meats paid for?'

'No.'

'Mr. Waite, do you know Trevor Heath?'

'Yes, I met Heath through Hammersley.'

'Mr. Waite, I have to ask you these questions,' Mr Howard said. 'Have you from time to time dealt in stolen goods?'

Waite, his hands resting on the edge of the witness box and looking a little uncomfortable, nodded.

'Yes,' he said quietly.

'Did Hammersley and Heath know that?'

'Yes, both.'

'Have you ever had any conversation with them about stolen goods?'

'Yes.'

'Can you recollect what either of them said to you about that?'

'Yes, it was put to me by both of them, knowing that I had contacts to shift large quantities of stolen goods. I was more or less made an agent. Nobody else knew about these stolen goods in the town.'

'If you bought any stolen goods, was there any conversation about that?'

'I only had stolen goods from London.'

'Why did you have stolen goods from London?'

Waite said the officers had told him he could get things stolen in any town but Brighton, because they wanted to keep themselves clear of complications locally. They would ask him if anybody had approached him to buy anything, and if it concerned something stolen in Brighton he would tell them about it. They never asked him about goods stolen outside the town.

Since his conversations with Heath and Hammersley he had received a quantity of stolen property at various times. It came from outside Brighton, and he had disposed of it. Both Heath and Hammersley knew he was doing it.

'Have you ever given any money to Hammersley?'

'Yes.'

'Was it given to him at regular intervals or at odd times?'

'Money at odd times, but meat and vegetables every week.'

'Have you ever given any money to Heath?'

'Yes, at odd times.'

'Did Heath have meat and other things too?'

'Yes.'

'Did they pay for the things they had each week?'

'They used to have two or three pounds worth of stuff, give me a ten shilling note and then wait for the change.'

'They asked for change?'

'No, they never asked for change, they just waited for it.'

Waite was then asked if he could give the court any kind of estimate of how much money he had given in all to Hammersley. He stood still for a few moments, looking into the air, his lips moving as if counting. He said that it was difficult over a period, but he thought it was about £200 in cash. Mr. Howard then asked if he could tell the value of the other things he had had.

'It would be very difficult. It would only be a rough guess.'

He was then asked how much money he had given to Heath.

'Not so much to Heath – about £50.'

'Did you ever give any money to Mr. Ridge?'

'No, sir, not personally.'

'I would like to move on to another subject,' Mr Howard said. 'Have you ever had possession of goods called Nescafé?'

'Yes.'

Here the three accused police officers all scribbled long notes.

Referring to stolen Nescafé, Waite said he had had a conversation with Hammersley and Heath after his first trial.

After you got the Nescafé did you want to get rid of it, to sell it?'

'Naturally. I explained to Hammersley alone about the Nescafé and was told that the man who had stolen it would be made the receiver.'

Some parts of Waite's evidence were inaudible to reporters and those sitting in the public seats. He was answering in little more than a whisper.

He said that at his first trial the jury disagreed, and when he was tried again he was acquitted. He stopped and took a few sips of water. His voice appeared a little stronger as he said that Hammersley told him about a man named Martin. He said that Martin had reported to the police that some Nescafé had been put in a hairdresser's shop. Waite said that he then went to see Martin to give him a rousting. He had known Martin slightly before Hammersley said something about him.

Waite then referred to thieves bringing some tobacco to him from the Brighton Co-operative Society shop. He bought the tobacco and paid £35, as near as he could remember.

'It was only a little quantity as I recall. I told Hammersley about the tobacco, and Heath was there when I told him.'

'Did you give either of them anything?'

'No, I informed them that they were going to do a big job. I told them about it.'

'Did you ever hear any more about the tobacco?'

'No.'

Waite said he sold the tobacco, adding that men named Spraggett and Mitchell were the two who bought it.

Mr. Howard asked, 'Do you know a jeweller's shop named Davis in Brighton?'

'Yes.'

'Have you ever had any conversation with Hammersley about the shop?'

'Yes, I told him the shop was going to be turned over for watches and that.'

'By 'turned over,' asked Mr Howard with a wry smile, 'do you mean robbed?'

'Yes.'

There were ripples of laughter in the court at this reply. The magistrates were seen to try to hide a smile with their hands.

'Heath was with Hammersley when I told them about this,' Waite continued. 'Spraggett and Mitchell had two or three places. They were living at Shoreham. They also had a room in Marine Parade.'

He said that he had this conversation with Hammersley and Heath about the jewellery going to be stolen in about 1955. Waite said that he didn't know the exact date on which the shop was to be robbed. Later he saw Hammersley, who told him he knew that Joan – that was Mrs. Watson – had been to the Marine Parade address. He also knew that Waite's telephone had been ringing all night long.

'He said the phone had been tapped and that I was lucky not to go and get the watches because he had several detectives with him.'

'Did anything happen to you regarding this jewellery business?'

'No, I never had anything to do with it.'

'Have you ever had a quantity of mixed groceries in your possession?'

'Yes.'

'Whose property was it?'

'Kearney and Tongue's.'

'Were these stolen groceries?'

'Yes.'

'How did they come into your possession?'

'They came by lorry.'

Another ripple of laughter ran through the court.

Waite said the groceries were put in various places – in his house, garage and outhouse. This was around Whitsun 1956.

After the goods had been delivered, Hammersley came to his home. The lorry that had been used belonged to one of Hammersley's friends (he didn't know his name), and Hammersley saw the goods in the house.

'Did he say anything about it?'

'Well, all he said was "I see you have got the goods all right". '

'Did he have any of them?'

'Yes.'

'What did he have?'

'He had some of everything – peaches, butter, bacon.'

He couldn't remember if he saw Heath while the groceries was in his house.

'Did you give any money to anybody?'

'Not at that time, when they first came. After all the groceries were sold, the gang of about six handling them came down for the money I owed them and I paid them.'

'Did you give any money to anybody else?'

'Hammersley had £50.'

Waite told the court that he had received more stolen groceries later the same year.

'They were delivered just before Christmas 1956, about 11 pm, in a lorry. The lorry was driven up his driveway. Six people were in it. I was expecting Libby's corned beef. Part of the lorry was unloaded. They first started unloading tins of tomatoes, and then tinned peaches. The unloading made a terrific noise, and while the unloading was going on I saw a police officer coming up the drive. I made an exit.'

'Was it a quick exit?' Mr Howard asked with a slight grin.

'Yes, very quick.'

(More ripples of subdued laughter.)

Waite said that he went up to a tenant's flat and stayed about an hour. When he came down again the lorry and the policeman had gone. The contents of the lorry had been left on the lawn.

'They stayed there until about 3 am and then I moved them to my outhouse.'

After receiving the load he didn't see Hammersley for some time, but about a week later Hammersley came to his house. Some of the stolen property was still there.

'Did you say anything to Hammersley about the policeman arriving during the unloading?'

'I told him about it and said that I was worried about the policeman calling. I told him the policeman had called, and wondered if he had made out a report. He said he would find out.'

'Did he see the tins of peaches?'

'Yes, he had some. He had several tins on several different occasions.'

Waite said that Heath used to come to the shop in New England Road, which was open then. Asked if anything else happened about the tinned peaches, he said that Hammersley had made a report. Two of the men working for Waite were taken to the town hall and questioned about the peaches.

'Were any proceeding taken against you?'

'There were going to be proceedings taken against me.'

'Have any proceedings been taken against you?'

'No, sir.'

Waite, thoughtful as ever and at times leaning on the edge of the witness box, told the magistrates that on August Bank Holiday Saturday he saw a man called Ackerman. Asked if he knew a man known as Ted Wyatt, he replied, 'He is a tobacconist really by trade, but he does bookmaking under the counter.' After the conversation with Ackerman he saw Wyatt and Ackerman and then went to see him again on the following Monday.

'About three days later I saw Hammersley in the shop. I said I had been offered a quantity of cigarettes. They were stolen cigarettes.'

'Did you say they were stolen?'

'Yes, they knew. Hammersley didn't say anything at this time.'

About five days later he saw Hammersley, who told him where the cigarettes had been stolen from.

'He said they were from Bishopsgate goods yard, and he told me one of the station detectives was suspect as being one of the people involved in stealing them.'

Several people had told him about the railway police being in Brighton, Hammersley being one of them.

'Having said the cigarettes were stolen at Bishopsgate, did he say anything else to you?'

'He said the railway police were going to come down, take me to London to try to see if I could find them.'

'Did you go to London?'

'Yes. Mr. Hammersley came for me on the Sunday morning and took me up to London. I think it was 18th August.'

'Where did you go?'

'We went to Petticoat Lane with one or two characters.'

'What were you looking for?'

'I showed him the places where other stolen goods were stored.'

Waite said that on the way back to Brighton; Hammersley went to see Mr. Moody, chief of the station detectives. While Hammersley was there, he waited about a hundred yards down the road, sitting in the car.

'Do you know a man named Richardson,' Mr Howard asked him, 'sometimes called Ricky?'

'Yes, Dicky or Ricky.'

Waite said that on the following afternoon, August 19th, he had a telephone call from Ricky, and that he in turn called Hammersley. He told him that he had just had a telephone call offering him some cigarettes, to which he replied, 'Good.'

'As a result of the telephone call I went to Hammersley's home. The cigarettes came in two cartons. Richardson brought them. One was of tens, the other in twenties. I identified a brown cardboard carton in which some of the cigarettes had come. There were 6,000 in each carton. I unpacked the cigarettes and took the carton to Hammersley's house.'

While he was there, he said, Hammsersley rang Moody. He heard the conversation. The cigarettes had been offered at £6.10s a thousand. Hammersley repeated what Moody said over the phone. Hammersley asked if it was all right for the informant to buy some at that price. Moody said it was all right and said 'buy the lot'.

'Hammersley said, "Buy a couple of cartons for now." I took the two empty cartons to Hammersley, because he told me not to part with the cigarettes until I got the money. When I took the two cartons, he was out, because I told him I would bring them up at 9.30pm. But I left much earlier, and I left them under the porch-way.'

Waite said he received some Old Holborn tobacco, which was brought by Richardson. He also brought 15,000 cigarettes in sacks, together with the 40lbs of tobacco. He had seen Hammersley before these goods were delivered.

'I let him know who was bringing the cigarettes. I told him it was Richardson. Hammersley said, "Oh my God, I can't have him around!" Hammersley was with Heath at this time, and Hammersley went on to say, "I must get out to Richardson right away to burn all the cartons".'

Mr. Howard said, 'Do you remember the day when police officers from Scotland Yard and railway officers searched your house and shop?'

'Very much, sir.'

'Did they find anything in your shop?'

'Yes, 36 pounds of tobacco.'

'Among the police officers, was Heath there?'

'Yes.'

'Was anything found in the house?'

'Yes, about 3,000 cigarettes.'

Waite went on to say that the cigarettes and tobacco were seized by the police and that he was taken to the police station. There Heath took a statement from him.

'While he was taking it, did he say something to you?'

'Mr. Moody was there, but when Mr. Moody left the room, Heath said, "Cut this statement as short as you can". Then he said "Carry on for a while when he comes back and then finish".'

'Were you told why you were to do this?'

'Heath said I shouldn't say too much, that's all.'

Waite said he saw Hammersley later that same day and again on the Monday morning. Hammersley had told him that Waite had made him look a fool, but that was all right – he could stand that.

Waite said that while he had the shop in New England Road a man called Jack Ketley helped in the shop and another man called William Watson also worked there, Watson was a lorry driver. A third man called Maher had also worked there, succeeding Watson.

He had been in the witness box for two and a quarter hours when John Bosley, for Charles Ridge, began his cross-examination.

In answer to his first question, Waite said that his memory was as good as anyone else's. Asked about the green dye which ministry of food officials put on meat unfit for human consumption, he said that if it was on meat the enforcement office didn't bother to look at it.

'Do you remember saying, "There are going to be proceedings against me, but Scotland Yard came in"?'

'I said I thought there would be proceedings. I wasn't charged. Mr. Hammersley wanted me prosecuted.'

Mr. Bosley then referred to newspaper reports, asking whether he had read them.

'Yes, very good reports, too.'

'Did you read what the solicitor general described you as?'

'Yes, I heard very well.'

'Did the solicitor general say you were a greengrocer, fruiterer and a poulterer, an undischarged bankrupt, a receiver of stolen goods and obviously a scoundrel?'

Mr. Maxwell Turner, for the prosecution, jumped to his feet, saying, 'He cannot know what the solicitor general said about him.

He was not in court. He can only read in the papers what was said about him.'

Mr. Bosley said very calmly, 'Is it correct to say that you read the papers about what the solicitor general said about you?'

Waite, equally calm, replied, 'I never read it. Someone told me about it. I didn't have to read it. I was reminded of it too much. I was told by so many people, I didn't have to read it.'

'When you heard what people said, did you not turn and look at the papers yourself?'

'No, I was too upset,' he said with a smile.

Mr. Bosley, now appearing a little annoyed, continued, 'I see you are smiling as you say that. Would the solicitor general be wrong in describing you as a greengrocer, fruiterer and poulterer?'

'No, I don't think so.'

'Would he be wrong if he described you as an undischarged bankrupt?'

Waite seemed to be expecting this question and replied to it gleefully, 'You should know that Mr. Bosley. You are the solicitor acting for the trustees.'

'Litigation?'

'You were once my solicitor,' Waite quickly replied.

Mr. Vokins, the chairman, said to Waite, 'Just answer the questions.'

'Would the solicitor general be wrong,' Mr Bosley continued, 'in describing you as a receiver of stolen goods?'

'How can he be wrong?' Waite answered.

David Peck, for Hammersley, asked Waite when he was given permission to buy stuff outside Brighton.

'When I was charged with the Nescafé. I kept my mouth quiet and seemed to come into favour.'

'When were you given permission to receive stolen goods from outside Brighton?'

'When I was told about certain commodities which I could get through a friend of Mr. Hammersley. This was sometime in 1952 or 1953.'

'How long have you been providing information for the police?'

'I have never provided information for the police. I have only given information to Mr. Hammersley because he more or less put me on to good things.'

'Over what period have you been giving information to the police?'

'Since Hammersley and I have been tied up together, about three or four years.'

Replying to Cyril Wheeler, for Heath, Waite said that a friend of Hammersley was in contact with an organisation of thieves in London. He added, 'I was the golliwog who disposed of the goods.'

He had disposed of stolen goods from the London organisation on two occasions. He was then asked about his salary for managing the shop in New England Road.

'I don't think it's any of your business,' Waite replied indignantly. 'I refuse to answer that question.'

Mr. J. Gwynne Thomas, the magistrates' clerk, told Waite, 'You cannot refuse to answer.'

Waite paused for a few seconds, looking towards the prosecution team, and then after a further pause answered, 'I do not receive a salary.'

When Mr. Wheeler continued with this line of questioning, Mr. Maxwell Turner intervened. A short conversation was held between counsel and the chairman. Mr. Vokins said to Waite, 'You need not answer anything that may incriminate you as an undischarged bankrupt.'

Waite replied, 'Thank you, sir.'

Waite agreed with Mr. Wheeler that the whole of the police investigation relating to the Nescafé transaction was carried out by West Sussex Police. Asked if he had received an informant's fee of £25 for giving information about a jeweller's shop robbery in Brighton, Waite answered, 'Sorry, sir.'

At this stage Waite asked for a glass of water and then drank it all down in one go. He then asked for another glass, and when the police sergeant brought it, he drank that down too without a break.

Waite agreed that Heath had said his statement about the cigarettes was too long, but he had made it as short as he could.

'Did Sergeant Heath conduct a search?' Mr Wheeler asked.

'I'm not supposed to know anything about that.'

Asked if Heath found 30lbs of Old Holborn tobacco, Waite replied, 'No, 36lbs.'

When asked if Sgt Heath and Supt Moody had gone to his house in Preston Road, Waite said, 'Correct, sir.'

Mr. Wheeler then asked if there were other officers there.

'I think half of the police force was there,' Waite replied.

He said the cigarettes were found in the front room and a few more in the bedroom.

Re-examining, Mr. Turner said, 'You have been asked whether you consider yourself a scoundrel and you have been asked whether you received stolen property and so on. I think we ought to know for what offences you have been convicted.

'Is it right that in 1933 you were fined £3 for stealing?'

'I can't remember.'

'In 1934 for stealing a handbag, two months hard labour?'

'No, not guilty,' Waite replied.

When Mr. Turner said he wanted to get the picture right, because the witness had been put forward as a villain, Mr. Bosley stood up.

'Yes, by you,' he remarked.

Mr. Turner said, 'I am not complaining.'

Waite, who had been leaning on the front of the witness box, stood up straight and said, 'If you say I am a villain, I will accept that.'

'Since 1940,' Mr Turner continued, 'have you ever been convicted of any dishonesty?'

'No.'

'Have you been, in fact, convicted of offences relating to the black market?'

'Yes, quite a number of them.'

This completed Waite's evidence, which had lasted in total for three hours and 27 minutes. The court then rose for the day and the first week of the trial ended, the magistrates having heard the evidence of 35 witnesses over the course of 25 hours.

Day Six

Monday 2nd December was a bitterly cold day, with north winds taking the temperature down close to freezing. This failed to prevent people queueing for the start of the trial's second week. The first of them were two elderly women, who arrived outside the main door of the town hall at 7 o'clock. With an hour to go before the court re-convened the crowd numbered around 80 people, all standing in an orderly queue, coat collars turned up, scarves tied tightly around faces.

As the opening time of the court approached larger numbers of police arrived, and people were shepherded into the court room in small numbers. Sharp at 10.30am the first witness was called.

Mrs. Joan Watson of Preston Road slowly made for the witness box. After she had taken the oath, permission was granted for her to sit down. She sat forward in her seat, hands clasped, and gave her name and address in a very quiet, barely audible, voice.

Mr. Maxwell Turner, for the prosecution, told her, 'I am afraid you will have to speak a great deal louder. It is not very easy to hear in this court.'

Mrs. Watson said that her address was the same as Ernie Waite's, and that she had been living with him for about five years. She said she had come to Brighton about seven years before, when she worked in a hotel as a receptionist. Waite was carrying on a business from that address. He supplied hotels with vegetables, fruit, poultry and meat.

'I knew Ridge, Hammersley and Heath,' she said. 'I have seen Ridge but have not been introduced to him, but I have met Hammersley on numerous occasions. I first saw him about four-and-a-half years ago, and first met Heath about the same time.'

'Were you able to tell the relationship between the accused and Mr. Waite?'

'Yes.'

Mr. Turner then asked her about the relationship between Waite and Ridge.

She started to say, 'I have heard him speak through another man of Ridge . . . ' but she was stopped by Mr. Turner.

'I never saw anything of Mr. Waite and Mr. Ridge speaking together,' she continued, 'but I saw and heard Waite and Hammersley talking together on a number of occasions. They were on very friendly terms.'

'And Heath, the same?'

'Yes, sir, very friendly.'

Mr. Turner then asked her if any of them used to come to the house. She said both Hammersley and Heath came every week for various things. She added, 'They didn't pay for them.'

Mrs. Watson said she opened a shop at no. 39, New England Road in September 1956. Hammersley and Heath used to come to that shop sometimes two and three times a week. She said, 'They came because they wished to speak to Mr. Waite on some occasions, but at other times they came for their vegetables and groceries.'

'When they came to collect groceries, did they pay for them?'

'No, sir, not always. If I served them they would give me a 10 shilling note and just wait there for the change.'

'What was the value of the stuff?'

'About £2.'

' 'After you opened the shop, did they still continue to come to the house and collect things or not?'

'No, sir, only at Christmas time.'

'What happened at Christmas time?'

'They came to collect some extra poultry and some tinned goods.'

'Did they come together or separately?'

'Separately, sir.'

'Did they pay for the extra poultry and tinned goods at Christmas time?'

'No.'

After every couple of questions Mr. Turner glanced at his papers on the desk. He told the bench that he wanted to ask Mrs. Watson about a number of specific cases.

'Do you remember an occasion when the Co-operative Stores in Lewes Road was broken into and cigarettes stolen?'

'Yes,' she said.

'What did you know about that case?'

'Well, I remember two men bringing cigarettes in a suitcase to the house at 155 Preston Road.'

'Did the cigarettes remain at 155 Preston Road?'

'Yes, sir.'

'Did Waite see two men?'

'Yes.'

'Do you remember another occasion when a jeweller's shop was broken into by the same two men?'

'Yes I do, but I don't recollect the name of the shop.'

'The next day, do you remember answering the telephone?'

'Yes, it had been ringing a lot the previous evening.'

'Tell me who it was who kept ringing up?'

'It was one of the two men who had taken the stuff.'

'Later on did you go to the house where the thieves were living?'

'Yes, I did.'

'Did you see the thieves or not?'

No, sir. They had apparently left.'

'That same evening, did you see anyone?'

'Yes, Mr. Hammersley and Mr. Heath came.'

'Did they come to your house?'

'Yes.'

'Did they start by having a conversation with Mr. Waite?'

'Yes.'

'After a little time did Waite come out of his room, and did he and you go back into that room and see Hammersley and Heath?'

'That's right.'

'What was it Mr. Hammersley said to you?'

'Mr. Hammersley turned round to me and said the conversation I had held with the thief over the telephone had been tapped.'

'What else?'

'And they had a tape recording of the conversation I had with the gentleman in question.'

'You say the gent in question. Do you mean the thief?'

'That's right.'

Mrs. Watson went on to say that Hammersley had told her she was very lucky not to have been taken in by the police at the house when she had called to see them.

'Naturally I was sort of amazed, and went out into the kitchen and made a cup of tea. Mr. Waite gave Mr. Hammersley some money so that no action would be taken about me.'

She told the court that she first met a man named Ackerman just preceding the Christmas before her youngest baby was born in March 1956. She was asked if she remembered an incident around Whitsun 1956 and she agreed that she did.

'Did you personally meet Ackerman in relation to those groceries?'

'Yes, sir.'

She said that she met Ackerman on the first occasion in London. She was with Waite. They went round behind Petticoat Lane to Quaker Street.

'We met Ackerman in a café and then he took us round to where they had a garage and a yard where they did repairs to motors and lorries. There were two sheds there.'

Mr. Turner, seeming deep in thought, asked, 'Was there anything in those sheds?'

'Yes, groceries and whole cheeses and sides of bacon. It was full up with the stuff.'

Asked if anyone else was there, she said there were two others besides herself, Waite and Ackerman, and there were also men working in the yard. She said Waite had a conversation and then, much later, a lorry arrived at the yard. The goods were loaded on to the lorry. Mrs. Watson said that she came back to Brighton with the lorry. Waite went ahead in the car. At that time, she said, there was a man called Bill Watson working for Waite. Back in Brighton, she, Waite and Watson unloaded the lorry. They put the things into the cellar and outhouses at the Preston Road address.

Mrs. Watson said they had not been able to load all the property on to the lorry and the remainder was brought down by Mr. Ackerman on Whit Monday. During the three days between the deliveries, Hammersley came to the house once. The groceries she had brought down were in a big garage and some were in the house. They had not been disposed of. Hammersley had a conversation with Waite.

'I was present at first. They started to talk about the goods that had been brought in and then I walked away. As far as I can recollect Hammersley said, "I see the stuff is in".

'On the Whit Monday there was some butter among the stuff that Ackerman brought down. On the wrappers was the name Kearley and Tongue.'

She said that she re-wrapped it in plain wrappers. Two days later, she said, she remembered Ackerman coming in the morning and Hammersley coming to the house with Heath. Waite had a conversation with Hammersley and Heath. Mrs. Watson said that she went into the room from time to time.

'The conversation was regarding the stuff we had in. On that occasion I cannot remember particularly what was said, but they were talking about the tinned goods and butter, etcetera.'

Mrs. Watson said she remembered a telephone call from Ackerman about the beginning of December the previous year. She spoke to Waite and then had another telephone conversation with Ackerman. She said she was expecting a lorry load of corned beef to arrive at the house, and Ackerman arrived in a lorry between 10.30 and 11 the same night. The lorry did not contain corned beef as expected. There were peaches (Libby's) and tinned tomatoes. The load was put on the lawn in front of the house.

'How many people were engaged in unloading?'

'They brought six men besides Ackerman and they did the unloading on to the lawn.'

'Did they do it quietly or not?'

'No, not particularly, no. While the unloading was going on a uniformed policeman arrived. Waite came indoors and went upstairs to the tenants flat above. The tins of tomatoes weren't unloaded, but the peaches stayed.'

'How many cases of peaches were there?'

She opened her arms sideways and lengthways to demonstrate the size of a case of peaches. There were 24 large tins to a case.

'Try to work out the number of tins to the number of journeys.'

There was a loud gasp in court when Mrs. Watson replied, 'Well, sir, I know it took us until four in the morning from about midnight. We were going continuously.'

Asked about what happened to the peaches, Mrs. Watson said that they had them in the house for a little while.

'Did either Hammersley or Heath come to the house while they were there?'

'They both came, separately.'

Mr. Turner then said that he wished to change the subject and asked her to talk about Ketley.

'Did a time come when he left your employment?'

'Yes.'

'After he left your employment, do you remember hearing him discussed by anyone?"

'Yes, by Mr. Hammersley and Mr. Waite.'

'What was said about Ketley by Hammersley?'

'That Mr. Ketley had gone down to the police and made a statement regarding the tins of peaches that he had helped unload.'

'What did Hammersley say about it?'

'As far as I can recollect he spoke to Waite regarding it and they went away. I was serving in the shop and I went on serving.'

'Did you hear Hammersley say anything else?'

'I can't remember.'

Mrs. Watson then said, 'Just before August Bank Holiday this year I had another telephone call from Ackerman, about Senior Service cigarettes.'

She and Waite went to see Ted Wyatt, who had a paper shop and tobacconists. During that time Ackerman rang up again and also came to the house.

'Waite couldn't take the cigarettes because he didn't have the money,' she said. 'I would have had to take them.

'Hammersley came to the shop twice while I was there during the week after Bank Holiday. I remember the occasion when Hammersley and Waite went up to London. I first knew they were going on the Friday before the Sunday they went. Hammersley spoke to me about the journey. He said "You don't mind if we go to London without you, do you?" and I said "No." '

The journey was on August 18th. They went to London by car.

'Mr. Hammersley drove to the house. The following day a man called Richardson came to my shop. He and Waite left in Richardson's car. Following a telephone call, I locked up my shop and went back to the house. When I got there I found Senior Service cigarettes in the kitchen, on the chair and table, and some in the passage. They were packed in cartons. These were not the only cigarettes that arrived at the house – some came every few days for about five days. Then there was a spell, and then some more came.

'The cigarettes were kept in the house, some in the lounge and some in the bedroom. While the cigarettes were there, Richardson and Hammersley came to the house, but not together. Hammersley saw the cigarettes, went into the lounge and mentioned a letter that had been received by Superintendent Williams. He said it was written by Mr. Wyatt.'

'Did he say what the letter was about?'

'Yes, Mr. Wyatt had said that he had been offered Senior Service cigarettes by Mr. Waite.'

'What did Waite say about that?'

Mr. Waite was most amazed the letter had been written, and to my knowledge that was about the first Mr. Hammersley knew about the cigarettes. This was told to us before Mr. Hammersley and Waite went up to London.

'This was before Hammersley and Waite went to London on the 18th August?'

'Yes, sir, it was either August the 13th or maybe the 14th.'

'You told us that Waite was amazed that this letter had been written. Did he say so to Hammersley?'

'Yes.'

'What did Hammersley say?'

'I don't know.'

'You have told us that Hammersley saw the cigarettes in the lounge. Did Heath come to the house at all? Did he see them?'

'I know he knew about them.'

'Did you ever know that the Railway Police were making inquiries in Brighton about the cigarettes?'

'Yes.'

'When did you first know about that?'

'I knew it when they came to the shop.'

'You mean when they executed the search warrant?'

'Oh no, before then.'

At five minutes past midday Mrs. Watson had been in the witness box for 95 minutes. Although she was still seated, she swayed and went very pale. A uniformed sergeant gave her a glass of water. She gulped that down and said that she felt a little unwell, and then asked if she could take a few minutes rest. Very unsteady, she was helped from the court by two officials.

At 12.30 pm, after the court had been adjourned for 25 minutes, the magistrates returned and the chairman, Mr. Vokins, announced that as the witness was still slightly indisposed, the court would be adjourned until 2pm.

When Mrs. Watson resumed her evidence she remained sitting in the witness box, holding a jar of smelling salts. A uniformed woman police sergeant sat beside her. Asked if she felt well enough to continue her evidence, she nodded.

'After the railway police began making inquiries in Brighton,' Mr Turner resumed, 'did you overhear a conversation between Waite and Hammersley about the matter regarding the railway police?'

'I didn't hear them talk about that.'

'Do you remember the search warrant being executed on Saturday 31st August?'

'Yes.'

'How long before that, before August 31st, was the last delivery of cigarettes made?'

'Two days.'

'Who brought them?'

'Richardson, sir.'

'What happened to the other cigarettes. Had they been disposed of or not?'

'Some had.'

'What happened to those cigarettes which Richardson brought a couple of days before the 31st?'

'Some were sent out - they were already sold - and some remained in the house.

'Had any tobacco, apart from cigarettes, been delivered to the house?'

'Yes.'

'What kind?'

'Old Holborn.'

'Who had delivered that?'

'Richardson.'

'What had been done with that?'

'It had gone round to the shop. Some of the cigarettes were put in a room used by a Mrs Dean. They were put there out of the way, because there were too many to leave lying around.'

'On August 31st were you in your shop when the search warrant was executed?'

She replied that Heath had shown her the warrant.

'Waite went upstairs with some of the officers, while Heath and three other officers remained downstairs with me.'

'Did he say anything to you?'

'Yes.'

'What did he say?'

'He was surprised that the tobacco had been found upstairs.'

Mr. Turner said, 'No, I was meaning while Waite and the other officers were upstairs.'

'Yes, by then the tobacco had been found. Someone came downstairs and said so.'

'What did Heath say?'

'He said that he was surprised it was found on the premises, and that he would have thought we would have had more sense than to have it there.'

'Were you worried about the position at home?'

'Naturally.'

'As to what might be found at home?'

'Yes, sir.'

'Did you say anything to Heath?'

'Yes, I said I wanted to get round home quickly and Heath said it was no use, there were officers there already.'

'Were you worried about the position of Waite?'

'Yes.'

'Did you say anything to Heath about Waite?'

'I asked Heath what I could do when I realised they were taking Mr. Waite away. I asked him if there was anything I could do for Waite.'

'What did he say?'

'He said I was to telephone to Richardson and Mr. Hammersley, who was then on leave, and tell them what had happened at the shop.'

Mrs Watson said Heath told her she could come down later on during the day and see if there was anything she could do, but after telephoning Hammersley. She should ask Hammersley what to do. She telephoned Hammersley and told him exactly what had happened at the shop, and that Heath had suggested she take the blame. Hammersley was 'most surprised' when she told him the shop had been searched. She said Heath had given her Richardson's telephone number but that she had forgotten it.

Hammersley gave her Richardson's number and told her that if she had not heard anything by 8 o'clock, she should then go down and do what Heath had told her to do. She telephoned Richardson and Hammersley and no one else. Waite had been taken to the police station and she remained in the shop. Later she telephoned the police station and spoke to Waite but was cut off.

'After you were cut off, did Heath telephone you?'

'Yes.'

'What did he have to say to you?'

'It was just to say it was all right so far, and Mr. Waite was all right.'

'What did Heath say as to why you had been cut off?'

'He said one of the policemen had cut us off because it wasn't conversation regarding business. After the search warrants were executed, both Hammersley and Heath continued to call at the shop from time to time but not as much as before. They called for up to a fortnight afterwards.'

At about 2.20 pm Mr. Turner asked her, 'Are you feeling all right?' She replied that she was, but a policewoman gave her a glass of water, from which she drank.

David Peck, acting for Hammersley, then rose to his feet to begin his cross-examination. Mrs. Watson was told that she need not answer any questions that might incriminate her, and she nodded.

When Ackerman first brought articles to the house, she said, she did not know he was a thief, although she knew the goods were stolen.

'You knew Waite was a receiver of stolen goods?'

She said quietly, 'Well that's a matter of opinion, isn't it? I knew he received goods, but he received them because most of the time he was made to receive them.'

Mr Peck, standing erect, looked at the magistrates and slowly removed his spectacles before turning once more to Mrs. Watson.

'And you knew the goods he received were stolen goods. Ackerman had produced these goods?'

'Some of the time I knew they were stolen.'

'You knew that the goods you brought down with you in the lorry from Petticoat Lane were stolen goods?'

'Yes.'

'And you were disposing of the goods, or some of them, through your shop?'

'Yes, some of them.'

She went on to say that after Whitsun, Hammersley and Heath came to the house in the afternoon.

'What did Ackerman come for, in the morning?

'For money.'

The magistrates, who had been listening intently to Mrs. Watson's evidence, concerned about her well-being, adjourned the court until the following day once she had completed her evidence.

Scotland Yard had announced strict security measures during the morning aimed at protecting the witnesses due to give evidence in the case, and uniformed officers cordoned off the town hall as the court rose.

A Scotland Yard car, driven by a detective inspector, mounted the pavement, stopping a few feet from the entrance to the police station. A burly detective sergeant from the Scotland Yard team shielded the smartly dressed Mrs. Joan Watson as, with a scarf over her head, she hurriedly got into the car and was quickly driven away.

Day Seven

On the Tuesday morning a Mrs. Knowles and her friend Mrs. Steel led the queue for seats in the court for the seventh successive morning. Mrs. Knowles arrived first with her camp stool, travelling rug, hot drinks and sandwiches a full three-and-a-half hours before the hearing began. Mrs. Steel, who had headed the queue on two mornings, ran her a very close second. Two hours before the hearing was due to start, more than a dozen people were in the queue, wearing thick clothes on another very cold morning. Policemen patrolled the town hall precincts and often stopped to share a joke or two with the people standing in the line.

The court started six minutes late, and the first witness (and the 41st so far) was William Page of Woodbourne Avenue in Brighton – and, incidentally, the father of pop singer Jill Day. He wore a smart camel overcoat and described himself as a commission agent.

He told the magistrates about a telephone interview he had with Ridge about the prosecution of somebody regarding betting premises. He thought it was in April of this year, at about 9.15 am on a Sunday morning. Asked if he would rather write down the name of the man concerned, Mr. Page said that he didn't mind giving it: the name was Tousson.

'I said to Ridge, "This is William Page speaking". He seemed hysterical. He screamed at me and said, "How dare you ring me at this time?" I asked him what time I could see him, and I said, "I want to see you tomorrow morning, name your own time." Ridge said, "11 o'clock".

'Next morning,' Page continued, 'I was shown into his office by a superintendent, and he said, "Take a seat, Mr. Page." The other gentleman was also told to take a seat, and I said to Ridge, "I don't want to speak to him. I've come here to speak to you personally." He then told Superintendent Hill to wait outside for a few moments, and then I took a seat.

'I said "You'll be rather surprised why I have come down here to see you. As a matter of fact, I have come down to help you clean up this town." He replied by saying, "But I never said the town wanted cleaning up." I said, "But I think it does, and that it why I'm here." I said, "Firstly, you know one of your officers has taken £50 off a person and had them convicted?" Mr. Ridge said, "Will you give me the name?" I said, "At the proper time and place." '

Page added that he asked Ridge why one of his top men interviewed a young lad he had helped. He asked, 'Why should this officer interview this lad before he goes off to work – for this firm?'

Replying to Gerald Howard QC, one of the prosecuting team, Page said, 'When I finished repeating the statement I have just made to you, he turned round and said, "Pagey, put your cards on the table and tell me what you want." '

'What did you say?' asked Mr Howard.

'I said, "You summoned a man for aiding and abetting me. This is a liberty, and this man has a wife and three children and is going into hospital with suspected cancer of the throat." '

Ridge, he said, had asked him what he could do. When Page said he didn't know what he could do, Ridge answered: 'Well, I can have a word with the magistrates' clerk and get him a maximum fine.'

Page said he didn't want that: why should this man have a conviction when Bellson's Club had been raided five times and the landlord had never had a conviction?

'What was Bellson's Club?' Mr Howard asked.

'The Burlesque Club.'

Page added that Tousson had not been prosecuted.

'After you had spoken about Bellson's Club,' Mr Howard continued, 'did you do something? Did you put something on the table?'

'Yes. Mr Ridge said to me, "This is going to be the first of the prosecutions." I put my hand in my pocket and I put £1 on the table and said, "I bet a pound you don't prosecute Leach, who was the owner of the Burlesque Club, and Davis, who is my official landlord." '

'Did Mr. Ridge say anything to that?'

'Just a second – I remember every word.'

Here Mr. Page paused for a moment, looking into the air, as if to fully recall the words: 'I then asked him why he had evicted me from three different premises. He said that it wasn't anything to do with him. I told him that it was.'

'You have been referring to Mr. Tousson,' said Mr Howard. 'Was he a relation to you in the sense of tenant or landlord?'

'Davis owns the premises. He leased the restaurant to Tousson and then Tousson was renting me the bottom room.'

Page agreed that during the conversation with Ridge he had mentioned someone called Kiki.

When Mr. Howard sat down, apparently concluding his examination, Mr. Page addressed the magistrates.

'There is one special question the gentleman hasn't asked me.'

Mr. Howard stood up and said, 'I have asked such questions as I desire to ask you.'

John Bosley (for Ridge) said, 'I should have thought the matter was concluded.'

Page, looking decidedly unhappy, glared towards the prosecution team and then left the witness box.

The next witness was Mrs. Olive Tarff, an attractive brunette, wearing a dark grey coat over an olive dress. Having taken the stand she said that her address was 155, Preston Road, Brighton. Answering Mr. Howard, she said she was separated from her husband and for the past four years had been living with William (or Bill) Watson. In 1956, she said, Watson was employed by Ernie Waite as a van driver.

She said that about Whitsun 1956 she remembered going back fairly late one evening and seeing a lorry in the drive. The following day she unwrapped and re-wrapped butter in her bedroom. It was brought to her room by Mr. Watson and Mr. Waite. The job of unwrapping and wrapping took her about three days. Here her evidence concluded.

The next witness, the 43rd, was Frederick Ketley. He wore a smart grey overcoat and a fawn coloured scarf. Having taken the oath. he said that he did not wish to disclose his address and handed a business card to the magistrates' clerk. He stated that he had his own business as a fruiterer.

In October 1956, he said, he had started working for Ernest Waite. He worked in his shop at 39, New England Road until the end of May 1957, as an assistant. One Sunday evening in December 1956, about 11 to 11.30, he was at Waite's house in Preston Road, Brighton, when a van arrived. He did not see the lorry itself, but he knew tinned peaches were taken off it.

The unloading made rather a noise and a police constable came. There were six men with the van and they all ran into the house, locking the door behind them. The cartons of fruit were later put in a room at the back of the house. After a short time they were taken to the shop and a certain number of tins were sold there. Early in January 1957, Hammersley and Heath came to the shop. Hammersley came first and Heath about a week later.

'I knew Heath as Trev. I went down to the CID building at the town hall to see him, to give him some information regarding the tinned peaches. This was in January but I was not able to see Trev. I did see him later in the shop, a fortnight or maybe three weeks later, after Waite was serving and I said to Heath, "I would like to see you if you have a few minutes to spare". Heath didn't acknowledge me at all.

'Three or four weeks later I went to see Trev, but I wasn't able to see him. Later on I went again to see him – this would be about August time – and eventually I saw Heath. He was standing inside the CID office. Heath took me to the end of the corridor and we went inside a room together. He said, "Have you come to see me about cigarettes?" I said, No, it was a different matter: peaches. I then told him exactly what I have told the court and he made a note of it. He took a statement from me, I signed it and he thanked me. I told him I had been trying twice before to get in touch with him and I had tried to speak to him in the shop.'

Later the same day Ernie Waite came around to Ketley's shop. He had a conversation with Waite, and then telephoned Heath.

'I explained that Mr. Waite had called around to my shop. I asked him how Waite knew I had been round to the town hall. Heath said, "Well, I haven't said anything." Heath said that in future I was to get in touch with Sergeant Johnson.'

Answering David Peck (for Hammersley) Ketley said that he started to work for Waite in October 1956 and left the following 27th May. Mr. Cyril Wheeler (for Heath) asked him whether, when he went to the CID office to see Heath in January 1957, he had given any reason for not seeing him. Ketley said, 'I didn't know till the day after what his name was. I said I wanted to see Trev.'

Mr. Wheeler continued, 'Whom did you see on the first occasion?'

'I saw a sergeant at the desk.'

'Did you see some other detective?'

'I didn't ask if I might see some other detective. I thought I might see the man I knew.'

'Did you leave any message at that time?'

'No.'

Ketley said that some six weeks or so later he went again to the CID office and saw somebody in plain clothes just outside the office. He said to him, 'Is Trev about?' and the man replied, 'Trev who?'

Ketley said he knew him only as Trev, so he went away. Finally, in August, he saw Heath and made a fairly detailed statement to him.

'Did you say that the tinned peaches were stolen?'

'I did explain there were six men with the lorry. He said "I wish I had known. If you had phoned me before I could have caught them at it." He made it clear he was anxious to have what information he could about Mr. Waite.'

'Did you tell him that all six men in the lorry were wearing gloves?'

'Yes.'

'And that had aroused your suspicious?'

'Yes.'

Ketley agreed that he had been given a tin of peaches by Waite and that he had mentioned this to Heath, who said, 'Don't part with that; it may be important.' He also said he had told Heath that a lorry had been stolen and afterwards abandoned at Redhill. Heath explained to him that Sgt Johnson had now been put on the inquiry regarding the tinned peaches.

Re-examining Ketley, Mr. Howard said, 'You were just asked and you said you spoke to Heath about those peaches, and he said "It's a pity you didn't tell me this before." When he told you that, did you say anything to him?'

'I said, "I tried to get in contact with you by going to the CID, but they didn't seem to grasp who I meant when I asked for Trev". I also told him I had seen him at the shop and asked to see him for five minutes.'

'What did he say?'

'He said he never had time to stop and talk.'

The following witness was a member of Brighton Police, PC Harold (Nick) Kerry. He told the magistrates that on December 9th 1956 he was on duty 20 beat, working nights.

Mr. Maxwell, prosecuting, asked, 'Do you remember an incident that took place on the night of Sunday 9th December?'

'Yes, I do.'

He said he heard a noise – banging and voices – in the neighbourhood of no. 155, Preston Road. He went to see what was going on and saw a lorry in the drive and a number of men.

'I recognised Mr. Waite. The men were either loading or unloading the lorry. At any rate they were paying attention to it. Whatever they were doing, they stopped when I arrived. They remained with the lorry but Mr. Waite went round to the house. I was only concerned with the noise that was going on. I spoke to somebody, and after that I left and continued on my beat.'

Pc Nick Kerry, who investigated the sound of the stolen food being unloaded.

The next witness, another Brighton police officer, was Det Sgt Robert Johnson. He said that on September 6th he had been shown by Hammersley a statement made by Ketley that morning and taken by Heath. The statement concerned an allegation that a load of canned goods had been delivered to Waite.

Afterwards, at about 6 pm on that same day, he and Heath saw William Watson. Before then Ketley had rung up the police station and he (Sgt. Johnson) had spoken to him. When he and Heath saw Watson no information was given that Ketley had supplied a statement to the police.

Mr. Turner said, 'So far as you knew, who *did* know that Ketley had made a statement to the police?'

'I knew, Heath and Hammersley knew.'

'Did you tell anybody that Ketley had made a statement to the police?'

'No.'

Mr. David Peck, for Hammersley, then rose to ask the detective sergeant a series of questions.

'When Hammersley gave you Ketley's statement did he tell you to investigate Waite and pursue this enquiry as hard as you could?'

'Yes, he did.

'When you saw Watson that evening, with Heath, were you able to take a statement from Watson?'

'Yes.'

'As a result of your enquiries did you establish that the goods, the peaches, were stolen or not?'

'I could not.'

'Could you find any report that peaches had been stolen at about that time?'

'No.'

'Or that a lorry had been stolen about that time?'

'No.'

'Or indeed that a lorry had been abandoned at Redhill about that time?'

'No.'

'As far as the police could discover, there were no stolen peaches?'

'As far as I could discover, there were no stolen peaches.'

Mr. Peck then took his seat.

Mr. Cyril Wheeler (for Heath) began his cross-examination by asking, 'You made all due enquiries, which proved abortive?'

'Yes.'

'Did you so report to your superiors?'

'Yes.'

'Would that be a written report?'

'It would.'

Sergeant Johnson said the documents relating to the tinned peaches were collected together in one file and placed in the daily occurrence file in the front office of the police station.

'As a result of the inquiry made into this matter, were you able to come to a conclusion as to where the peaches came from?'

'None at all.'

'Nor whether Waite, who received them, had paid anybody for them?'

'No.'

Sgt Johnson said that when he and Heath decided to interview Watson a message was sent to the market, where Watson was working, asking him to come over to the CID office. He did not know who sent the message. He thought Watson arrived at the CID office about 6 pm. Heath suggested they should send for Watson – he said he had helped them before, or words to that effect.

The next witness was Frank Maher of Goodwood Way, Brighton. He began his evidence by saying that he used to work for Mr. Waite as a shop assistant and also as a van driver. About the end of May he was arrested by Heath and charged with office breaking. At Brighton quarter sessions he was placed on probation. Afterwards he started working for Waite.

'After I started working I saw Heath in Waite's shop at 39, New England Road. Heath mentioned the fact that I had one man to thank for getting me out of a prison sentence. I was led to believe it was Waite. It had been voiced around that he would help me. Heath said, "Treat him right." I saw Heath once a week in the shop. He came there for groceries and I also saw Hammersley there. Hammersley also came once a week for groceries, but they came separately.'

Mr. Maher said he knew a man called Richardson who had a shooting brake, and he remembered an occasion when he saw the vehicle in the drive at 155 Preston Road.

'I went into the house then and saw in the passage by the stairs two sacks. After that I noticed a lot of Senior Service cigarettes lying around.'

Cross-examined by Mr. Peck, he said he was at Preston Road every day but never lived there. Then Cyril Wheeler rose from his seat, and in further cross-examination Maher said that he had been charged with two separate charges of office breaking and theft. The theft charge was in connection with some TV cable.

'Did you know it was as a result of information given to the police by Waite that you were charged with that offence?'

'No.'

Maher agreed that he was charged with an offence concerning Sussex Canners and that he discussed that with Waite after he had committed the offence. Asked about Heath's visits to the shop, he said he had never actually served him, but he had been present a number of times when Heath was served by someone else.

'Have you ever seen him pay money?'

'I have seen money change hands, yes.'

Maher was then asked if he had seen Hammersley in there as well. He said that he had. He had also seen money pass hands on those occasions.

At the conclusion of his evidence and cross-examination the magistrates adjourned for lunch. For the afternoon session the public gallery was again full.

The first witness after lunch was Edward Wyatt, a newsagent and tobacconist of 58, Upper Gloucester Road, Brighton. He told the court that in August 1957 he had a conversation with a man named Chapman. Afterwards, but not immediately, he wrote a letter to Supt Williams of Brighton Police. He identified a piece of paper that was handed to him, agreeing that the letter had a date stamp of August 6th.

Mr. Maxwell Turner, prosecuting, then read from a piece of paper in his hand: 'G. Waite of Preston Road is trying to dispose of cigarettes, Senior Service, 169 cases, 600 a case, over a million cigarettes, wholesale price £9,000. They are in a 2-ton Bedford outside town and intend to deliver to purchaser, by-passing Waite. I think the quantity is too large for any local wholesaler to handle and I don't think they would buy them, as they are far too respectable. The only chance is to wait for the Bedford or any other means at their disposal. I don't think anybody else has been approached, but keep me out of it.'

Answering Mr. Turner, Wyatt agreed that the letter had been originally written upon a piece of paper with his letter heading: this had been torn off.

Mr. Bosley (representing Ridge) said, 'If we are going to have letters read out by somebody, as sent out by some third party to other third parties, that is no real evidence against the defendants.'

Mr. Howard said evidence would be brought later which would, in their submission, make the letters proved.

After solicitors had read the letter, Mr. Turner produced another piece of paper and asked Wyatt, 'Is this yet another letter which you wrote to Supt Williams, dated August 11th?' Wyatt studied the piece of paper, looked up and nodded. Mr. Turner then read from this second piece of paper. Much of what he said was inaudible to the reporters and to many sitting in the public gallery. One man made a point of leaning forward and cupping his hand to his ear.

The next witness was Superintendent Edwin Moody from Liverpool Street Station in London, the first of the railway police to be giving evidence. Having taken the oath, he looked straight at the magistrates and said that during the first week of August he learned of the theft of a trailer containing 305 cartons of cigarettes from Bishopsgate goods depot. On August 8th he sent a railway police officer, Det Sgt Spiers, to make inquiries of Brighton Police. As a result of his report, he on August 9th sent Spires and Det Insp Wright to Brighton, and on August 14th he decided to take a personal part in the investigations.

He said that when he got to Brighton he met Heath in the Caxton Public House at 36, North Gardens. He was accompanied by Det Insp Wright and Det Insp Hendy, both members of the

Transport Commission Police. No other member of Brighton Police was present. The three railway officers and Heath had lunch together. At that time he didn't know which Brighton officer had the cigarettes inquiry in hand, but during lunch Heath told him that Hammersley was responsible.

After lunch, they went to Brighton CID headquarters and at 5pm Supt Williams came in.

'Heath, Wright, Hendy and I were present at this time. I was introduced to Superintendent Williams and told him, "I am going to take a personal part in this investigation".'

The court listened eagerly as Superintendent Moody told how Supt Williams left the office and came back a few minutes later with two envelopes. Heath was present at this time. Supt Williams took a letter out of one of the envelopes.

'I noticed it was folded into three. He folded the top third part of the letter back, and as he did so, I noticed it had a name in thick black print, beginning with a "W". Superintendent Williams looked at the contents of the letter and quoted from it. Heath was there all the time and could hear what was being said. Quoting from the letter Superintendent Williams said, "169 cases of cigarettes have been offered in Brighton. They were brought to Brighton. They were left outside the town on a lorry. They had nowhere to put them. I wish we had known: we would have put them somewhere." No names were mentioned and Hammersley was not present at that time.'

Supt Williams had told him, 'Hammersley has the inquiry – I know little about how far it has advanced.'

Hammersley arrived about 6 pm and they were introduced. Hammersley told Moody that he had a reliable contact. A telephone message was received at the contact's house at midnight on 1st August. He later received a visit and he was offered 169 cases of cigarettes at £6.10s a thousand. This was too big for this contact to handle. The contact offered to find someone who would take them.

Supt Moody said Hammersley had added, 'After Inspector Wright's visit on the 9th, I got the contact to go to London and see if he could find out where the cigarettes were. He went to the Three

Archers public house in the East End of London where he met Ackerman and another man. They made their way to the Elephant and Castle and the contact knows where the cigarettes are.'

Supt Moody said Hammersley described the location, and he took notes of it. Hammersley said that his contact was fully reliable, and 'He will do anything if you show him a pound.'

Moody had then introduced the question of a reward, saying, 'Well, there is £15,000 involved. I think I can mention the sum of £500 as a reward.'

He said that he left Brighton that evening and he had not been told the name of the contact.

Continuing, Supt Moody said, 'On August 15th I went to Southwark police station, where I met Inspector Butler and Sergeant Vibart of the Metropolitan Police.'

'You told us you made notes of a certain area described by Hammersley?' Mr Howard asked.

"Yes."

'Where did you go with these officers?'

'We went to a location indicated near the Elephant and Castle by Hammersley.'

'Did you find anything of any interest there?'

'There were so many places similar to that described that we gave the search up as useless.'

'Next day, did you go to Brighton again?'

'Yes, I went to the CID headquarters of Brighton.'

'I think you found Hammersley was at home and he was telephoned.'

'We met him at the corner of Glen Rise and the main road. I was accompanied by Inspector Wright and Inspector Hendy.'

Supt Moody said that Hammersley then got into the car with them and he then went on to describe a conversation they had.

'I cannot remember the exact words I said to Hammersley, but I think it was something like "the information concerning the Elephant and Castle was useless," and I told him why. I said, "There were so many similar places it was impossible to find the place you referred to." I then said to him, "Who is your contact?" He said, "I'm not going to tell you." I then said, "I think the best arrangement would be for your contact to go to London and I will follow him up in a car to the location."

'Hammersley said, "No, he won't have that; he does other business in London which he wouldn't want the police to know anything about." I became insistent that something should be done, and Hammersley said, "Suppose I come to London with the contact and see the place, and then I can describe it to you." I agreed. Hammersley then said, "But how are we to get there?" I said, "I can give you two free passes to travel by train." He said, "No, the contact won't travel by train."

'I then said, "Let him use his own car and I will pay the expenses." Hammersley said, "No, the gang knows his car and he wouldn't want it to be seen." Inspector Hendy chipped in and said, "Well, have this one," – indicating the car we were sitting in. Hammersley said, "No, you know this car – you'll pick it up in London and follow it." I said, rather indignantly, "I will do no such thing," but he wouldn't accept my assurance.'

Moody had then offered to pay for the hire of a car, and Hammersley had accepted this. It was agreed that he would travel on Sunday August 18th.

'Was there any further conversation about the contact?' Mr Howard asked.

'He then mentioned the Montpelier Hotel and said, "Some of your stuff went to the Montpelier. But they only had one case. There are only about 1,000 cigarettes left. They will be mixed up with their ordinary stock and you wouldn't identify them. It's no use you making inquiries into that." I said to Hammersley: "'It's obvious that your contact knows where the cigarettes are and I want to get my hands on those cartons." Hammersley answered by saying, "You'll find out on Sunday." I said, "It's about time the two sides were brought together -- your contact and mine." That ended the conversation.'

Before leaving Hammersley, Moody had said, 'On your way back from London you'll have to pass near Ewell, where I live. Why not telephone me or, better still, come and see me at home so that I can get the information quickly and do something? He had agreed to do one or the other.

On Sunday August 18th, Hammersley came to his home at about midday. He said that he had left the contact in the hired car about 70 yards down the road. They had been to the site at the Elephant and Castle, and Hammersley had made a rough sketch of the place. Moody then produced the sketch on a tattered piece of paper.

Hammersley said the goods were in a BRS depot and then went on to describe another place with double brown doors nearby and said 'Some of your stolen stuff goes there but not the cigarettes.' He continued, 'I have been to Ham Park Road. I saw Ackerman outside his house cleaning his car. It's a stone coloured Ford Consul OLA 853. We didn't stop – the contact ducked down as we passed. We stopped further down the road by a telephone box. The contact phoned Ackerman and I listened in.

'The contact asked Ackerman if there were any cigarettes going and Ackerman said they were all sold on Saturday at a knock-down price. The contact told Ackerman that he wanted some, and Ackerman said he would try and get some back.

'We went to Adler Engineering Works in Quaker Street, just behind Petticoat Lane. Some of your stolen stuff goes there. I met some of the gang and I posed as a hotel manager out to buy cheap.'

Moody told Hammersley that he knew the place and that it was searched the day after the theft. Hammersley said they were going to have another load in a fortnight's time, and asked, 'Why not leave everything until then, and then you can get the goods and the thieves. My contact is going to have the first offer.'

Supt Moody said they discussed that, and finally he said he was not waiting for anything else and was getting on with the job. He said that he watched from his front room window and saw Hammersley get into the driving seat of a car in which another man was seated. He could not recognise him.

Moody continued, 'After that, myself and Inspector Wright of the Railway Police and Inspector Butler and Sergeant Vibart of Scotland Yard, went to the BRS depot, indicated on the rough sketch on the afternoon of Sunday the 18th.'

He continued, slightly raising his voice, 'It was obvious on entering that no vehicle had ever been taken into the place. It was a bombed depot, rubble and rubbish was lying about, inches thick. There were some converted stables inside, converted into offices, and dust and debris showed nothing had ever been taken there.' He said he looked around the area described in the sketch and saw the place that had been described as having double brown doors. 'It was locked and bolted and we could not get in.'

Mr. Cyril Wheeler for Heath then began his cross-examination. Supt Moody said he had tried without success to find out the name of an informer known to Hammersley. Heath had told him that he did not know the name of the informer. Moody agreed that Heath had said to him, 'Why don't you "knock" Hammersley's informer?' In answer to a further question from Mr. Wheeler, Moody said that "knock" meant arrest. He added, 'My reply was, "I don't know him."'

Heath had then suggested that he 'tail up' Hammersley.

During the final hour of the day's court session, Supt Moody was under constant questioning from the defence team but kept perfectly calm. He said after one question, that the day after he had been to the BRS depot in Meadow Row, London on a useless search for stolen goods, he went down to Brighton, where he saw Det Supt Williams. Williams telephoned Hammersley and Moody spoke to him.

'I told him the result of our search at the BRS depot in Meadow Row. I said, "I think we've been taken for a ride." He said, "I don't understand this. This informant has never let me down before and he won't this time. I'm busy now, but I will see you at seven o'clock."

'While I was in Superintendent Williams' office, Heath came in. I said to Williams and Heath, "Hammersley mentioned the Montpelier," and I told them what he had said. I said there was no harm if we went over and had a look.'

Moody, Heath and Inspectors Wright and Hendy went by car to the Montpelier. Hammersley had said that he overheard a telephone conversation between someone and his contact. The caller had offered 30 cases of cigarettes. Later, Supt Moody said that he asked Hammersley where the cigarettes were going to be delivered. Hammersley said they could be put in a garage and then added that "They want £6.10s a thousand. Do you want them?'

Supt Moody had replied, 'What – buy back stolen property?'

In the evening Hammersley came to the CID office and told Moody that he didn't like what he said over the telephone.

'I said, "Do you think *I* like it, bringing men out on a fool's errand, being taken for a ride, because that's what it was." Again I asked who Hammersley's contact was. Hammersley said, "I'm not going to tell you. I wouldn't tell the superintendent or the chief constable. He's not only my informant, he's also my friend. I visit his home and he visits mine. He has done me many good turns. I'm not going to lose him. I know that if I told you, you'd be laughing. You'd be 50 miles away and I live here and have to get my living." '

Supt Moody said that just before he drove to the railway station to return to London, Hammersley had asked him, 'What about a sweetener for the contact? He hasn't had anything yet?'

Accused: the deputy head of Brighton CID, John Hammersley (right), is accompanied to court by Det Ch Insp Millen of Scotland Yard.

Hammersley suggested £10, but Moody told him, 'We'll see about it later.' Moody later said that he decided to send a detective to Brighton – under cover – without informing Brighton Police what he was doing.

DC Cook went to Brighton and on August 30th. After a conversation with him on his return, Supt Moody went with several other officers to Brighton. He detailed a number of officers to do various things.

'I sent two to watch 155 Preston Road and two to watch 37 New England Road – Spencer's tobacconists shop.'

On August 31st he said he obtained search warrants on these premises. He went with Heath and two other officers to 39 New England Road, and at that time he still did not know who Hammersley's contact was. Heath pointed out one of three people in the shop and said, 'That's Waite.'

The shop was closed, and the police found some Old Holborn tobacco in two cases or crates in the front room upstairs. Superintendent Moody said he went around to 155 Preston Road and found some Senior Service cigarettes in the front lounge. Waite was taken to the police station. There, he saw Hammersley and Sgt Vibart of the Metropolitan Police. Vibart said to Hammersley, 'This fellow Waite is your informant.'

Hammersley hesitated, but then said, 'Is he?'

Sgt Vibart said to Hammersley, 'You are a senior officer to me, but if that's your attitude I've got nothing further to say.' He then walked away. While he was there the chief constable, Mr. Ridge, came in. They had some conversation about the case, and then Mr. Ridge said, 'Well, good luck, I hope you get the ---.' He then left.

On September 2nd, as a result of a telephone message, Supt Moody went to CID headquarters, where he sawRidge. He hadn't asked to see him. He told Ridge the whole story he had just related to the court. When he finished Ridge said, 'I've got something to say to Hammersley. I can't understand why he went and saw Waite.'

Supt Moody said Ridge continued, 'I want you and all other officers who come to Brighton to feel happy in the knowledge when you leave that you have been speaking to officers in my force in whom you have complete confidence. If you have not that confidence then come to me or Mr. Williams. I shall always be available.

'You know, Moody, when you are dealing with thieves you have got to think their way, and to think their way you have got to know their ways, and to know their ways you have got to mix with them. I was brought up in the CID, but thank God I'm divorced from that now.'

Supt Moody said that Ridge added, 'I want things run this way,' (making a squaring motion with his hands), 'not this way' (making a criss-cross motion).

Mr. Peck (for Hammersley) said, 'You told us that you had a conversation with Mr. Ridge on September 3rd. Did you go back to London after that conversation?'

'Yes, sir, that day.'

'Did you receive a statement from Inspector Hammersley on September 4th or 5th?' asked Mr Peck, holding a three page document in his hands. 'Did that set out in outline what had transpired between you and him regarding Waite?'

'Yes.'

Supt Moody examined Hammersley's alleged statement and then said, 'There is one part of this statement that is not accurate. It says the officer required some empty cartons. I did not require empty cartons. I wanted two full cartons.'

Mr. Peck pointed out that the statement was dated September 3rd, 1957, and was made by Hammersley at Brighton.

'The object of the statement was with a view to prosecuting Waite, wasn't it?'

'No, not to my knowledge, sir.'

Mr. Peck then read the statement. When he had finished, Supt Moody said that it was also inaccurate when it referred to Hammersley's journey of the 18th. Hammersley said in the statement that on that journey he supplied Supt Moody with the name of the Montpelier Hotel in Brighton.

'In fact he gave me the name before that.'

At this moment the lid of a writing bench at the back of the court slammed down with a very loud bang, and the defendants, counsel and solicitors all jumped involuntarily.

David Peck then concluded his cross-examination with Supt Moody. After a short break, and after taking a few sips of water, the officer indicated that he was ready for further cross-examination.

Answering Mr. Wheeler (for Heath), he agreed that except for the visit to the Montpelier Hotel and the execution of the warrant Heath had played a minor part in this inquiry. Supt Moody went on to say that three search warrants were issued altogether, and a total of some twelve officers went to the searches. Heath went with him to 39, New England Road.

'Is it right to say,' Mr Wheeler asked, 'that Sergeant Heath made a suggestion to you? Did he say that was where you were most likely to find Waite?'

'He didn't tell me that,' Supt Moody replied. 'Somebody did, but he didn't.'

Supt Moody said that at 39 New England Road it was Heath who found the Old Holborn tobacco and called him into the room. Heath saw Waite and took a statement from him. Waite had been arrested by Heath.

The superintendent was asked whether any final decision had yet been made as to whether Waite would be prosecuted in connection with that particular matter. He said that Waite would not be prosecuted with regard to the cigarettes and tobacco found at New England Road and Preston Road.

He then read a report made by Heath about the searches carried out at New England Road and Preston Road. The report said that 384 ounce packets and 216 smaller packets of Old Holborn tobacco, making a total of 30lbs, were found. At Preston Road 1,360 cigarettes were found.

'As we know,' continued Mr Wheeler, 'you tried to find out the name of the informer and did not succeed. Did Sergeant Heath tell you that he didn't know the name of the informant?'

'He told me he didn't know.'

'Do you remember on one occasion Sergeant Heath suggesting

to you or saying that some effort should be made to find the informant's name and if necessary follow him?'

'What he said was this: "Why don't you knock Hammersley's informant?" '

Mr Wheeler said sharply, 'I don't find that very illuminating.'

Supt Moody replied, very calmly, 'It means, "Why don't you arrest him?" My reply to him was, "I don't know him."

'He then said, "You can soon find out." I asked how? He answered me by saying, "Tail up Hammersley."'

Supt Moody agreed with Mr. Wheeler that when he went to the Montpelier Hotel with Heath, Heath looked through the hotel register, found Ackerman's name and showed it to him. When his evidence came to a close, at lunch time, he had been in the witness box for a total of three hours and ten minutes.

The first witness after lunch was Det Sgt George Spiers of the British Transport Commission Police from Bishopsgate Station in London. He said that on August 8th, 1957, he went to Brighton to investigate the theft of a quantity of cigarettes and tobacco from Bishopsgate goods yard.

'I went to Brighton CID headquarters and there saw Sgt Heath. I told him I had called to see if he could help me in tracing a large quantity of cigarettes stolen from BTC premises at Bishopsgate Station during the night of 1st and 2nd August.

'He said, "Yes, would there be about a million and a half cigarettes involved?" I said, "Yes." Sgt Heath said, "Would they be mostly Senior Service?" Det Sgt Spiers said he agreed and had said there was also a large quantity of Old Holborn tobacco.

Then, he added, Heath had said, 'I think I can help you. My superintendent has received a letter from a friend who has been offered that amount of cigarettes. My superintendent spoke to me about it this morning.' Det Sgt Spiers said that at that point Heath left him to see the superintendent and on his return said that his superintendent was not available that morning owing to a race meeting. He said he gave Heath all the particulars concerning the theft of the tobacco. They mentioned informants, and Sergeant Heath asked, 'Do your people pay informants?'

Det Sgt Spiers said his superintendent would have no objection to paying someone who could help to recover the property or convict the thieves, and then he added, 'I think on my authority I can say £50 or more would be easily forthcoming.'

The following day he came back to Brighton in company with Det Insp Wright and they saw Heath in the police office at Brighton railway station.

Wright said to Heath, 'I understand you have some useful information concerning tobacco lost from our place at Bishopsgate station?' Sergeant Heath said, 'Yes, we have. It looks like your tobacco.'

Wright asked, 'How many cartons are there in Brighton?' but Heath didn't know. Wright then asked Heath, 'Who is your inform- ant working for you?'

Sergeant Heath replied, 'He works with my governor, Inspector Hammersley, whom I work with very closely. I don't think you will see him today. He isn't available.'

Det Sgt Spiers told Mr. Turner, prosecuting, that Heath said he did not know the name of the informant, but the informant would 'expect something.' Insp Wright had a telephone conversation with Hammersley when Spiers was present. Wright had asked, 'Can you see the informant and get something out of him?'

When the conversation ended Insp Wright came straight off the phone and said: 'He tells me 75 cartons have been flogged in London and there are still 169 still in Brighton.'

Cross-examined by Mr. Wheeler, Det Sgt Spiers agreed that Heath had given him all the help he could when he went down to Brighton on August 8th.

Mr. Wheeler spoke about buying information and asked Det Sgt Spiers, 'I suppose it's quite usual to buy information?'

'It's not unusual.'

'Would it be right to say it is not unusual for informants to be interested in what they are going to get out of it?'

'Quite correct.'

That ended Det Sgt Spiers' evidence, and he stepped down from the witness box.

Mr Vokins, the chairman, now suggested that the court adjourn until the following day. The local press reported that the magistrates appeared tired, and this may have been the reason the proceedings finished a little early that day.

Day Eight

Wednesday 3rd December started brightly but with a chill in the air. The usual people arrived early, but on this occasion the two knitters were pipped to the post by a middle aged man who stood reading his newspaper and seemed somewhat smug to be the first person in the queue. Soon all three were happily chatting among themselves.

Once again the public gallery was full by the time the magistrates entered the court, as 'Stand!' was called by the usher.

The day's first witness was Detective Inspector Leonard Wright, smartly dressed in a grey suit, white shirt and a blue tie. He stated that he was a member of the British Transport Commission Police at Liverpool Street. He said that on August 9th he went down to Brighton police station where he saw Heath and told him he understood he had some information regarding Senior Service cigarettes that were stolen from Bishopsgate goods station.

Heath replied 'Yes, it's quite right. They are certainly your cigarettes, without any doubt.' Later Heath asked him, 'What about the information. I suppose he will be rewarded for any work he does?' Insp Wright replied, 'Yes, the fairest way is surely payment on results.'

He then spoke to Hammersley on the telephone and said to him, 'This is a very serious theft, and I would appreciate all the help you can give.' Hammersley answered, 'Yes, I'll get my informant at work and assist all I can. You won't expect the informant to work for nothing?' Insp Wright had replied, 'Certainly not. Payment by results should meet the case.' Hammersley then said, 'Seventy-five of the cartons have been flogged in London. I'll keep in contact with you by telephone.'

Insp Wright said that at 2.15 pm the next day he was at Bishopsgate goods station when Heath telephoned and said he was speaking to Hammersley. The informant would be going to London on Sunday August 11th. Heath told him that the informant would meet the gang in a public house in the East End. He would try to buy ten cartons as an act of faith. He would also offer a price for whatever property might be left.

'If he is successful,' Heath said, 'the Commission will have to pay the money. I will phone you again.'

Insp Wright said that on August 12th Hammersley spoke to him on the telephone and said that all the cigarettes had been sold. Hammersley said his informant had told him the cigarettes were 'hot', and sold at knock-out prices.

Hammersley then said, 'The informant will be ringing the leader in London today at 1.45 pm and I shall try to be present.'

Detective Inspector Wright said that Hammersley phoned him again the following day at about 9.30 in the morning, saying the informant was still going to try and buy the ten cartons, and if successful they should have them about 2.30 to 3 pm and the informant would fetch them from town.

'I reported all these matters to Superintendent Moody,' the inspector said.

On August the 14th Supt Moody and he came down to Brighton and saw Heath in the morning. Heath told them that Hammersley was in charge of the inquiries at Brighton. Heath said that Hammersley would be on duty at about 6 pm that evening. At about 5 pm they went to Brighton CID headquarters and Insp Wright said he saw Supt Williams in the presence of Heath and Supt Moody.

Supt Williams left them almost immediately and returned quickly with two envelopes. He took a letter out of one, which he read, but not to the others. It said that '169 cartons of Senior Service cigarettes are on a lorry on the outskirts of Brighton. They apparently have nowhere to put them. We would have found a place for them if we had been told.'

Insp Wright said that when Supt Williams produced the letter he turned the top down, which prevented the name from being seen. The letter had a tradesman's bill heading across the top. At about six o'clock, said the inspector, Hammersley arrived and was introduced to Supt Moody. Hammersley said he had got a reliable informant and they ought to get somewhere.

The inspector, continuing his evidence, further described the location of a garage adjacent to the Elephant and Castle in London, saying 'The cigarettes were stated to be in the garage. On August 15th I and other officers tried to find that garage. We had been given a description where it was, but we were unable to find it.'

The next day he and Supt Moody came to Brighton again. Hammersley had begun his annual leave that day, and Moody arranged to meet him near his home.

'Myself, Superintendent Moody and Detective Inspector Hendy went by car to the meeting place and Hammersley got into the car.'

Moody told Hammersley they could not find the garage and they would want further details of the correct location. He said, 'I must insist we get somewhere in this investigation.' Hammersley replied, 'I'm prepared to go to London with the informant and locate them. How do we get there?' The superintendent said, 'I'll give you two first class railway passes.' Hammersley said, 'The informant doesn't travel by train.' Moody asked if he could go in his own car, and Hammersley replied, 'No, while going to London for this specific purpose he has other things to do in London which he would not care for the police to see.'

Det Insp Hendy said, 'You can take my car,' indicating the car in which they were sitting, but Hammersley immediately answered by saying, 'Oh no, my informant wouldn't agree to that because you would tail my informant in London.' Moody then suggested that Hammersley might hire a car and that he would pay for it. Hammersley agreed to that suggestion.

On Sunday, August 18th Insp Wright said he met Supt Moody, Insp Butler and Sgt Vibart at Scotland Yard and they went to the BRS depot in Meadow Row. He said, 'We entered the premises, which were bombed and disused. It was clear to us that no vehicles of any description had been in there for a very long time. The vegetation in the middle of the premises was about 4ft high.'

They made a thorough search of the whole premises and it was evident that nothing had been there. The search was abandoned.

The next day he and Moody again went to Brighton. Moody spoke to Hammersley on the telephone, and afterwards Heath took them to the Montpelier Hotel. Then they returned to the CID office where Moody had a further telephone conversation with Hammersley. At the end of this conversation Moody said to one of the officers, 'I don't believe Hammersley's story.'

Supt Moody said Hammersley had told him he could not understand it and that his informant had never let him down before. Hammersley had told him that while he was at the informant's place the telephone rang and the informant put his hand over the mouthpiece and whispered to him, 'I've been offered 30 cartons of Senior Service cigarettes and the Commission can have these if they buy them.'

Supt Moody then said, 'I'm not buying back our own cigarettes, which have been stolen.'

At 7 pm that same evening Hammersley came to the CID office and the arrangements were made that Hammersley would get two cartons from his informant and he might get them back in time for them to take back to London.

The chairman of the magistrates, Mr. Vokins, suggested that this would be a convenient time to adjourn for lunch.

Det Insp Wright continued his evidence when the afternoon session began. He said that Supt Moody told Hammersley, 'For God's sake let's have a bit of faith in each other. I am not concerned with your informer. I want to contact his contacts and trace back from there. We're all in this game together. We've got to break this job and it is down here in Brighton where this can be done.'

Hammersley replied, 'Why not wait and see what turns up from the two cartons when you get them back in London?'

Hammersley then made three telephone calls to find out if the cartons had been delivered. He came back to say that they had not been delivered yet.

Insp Wright said that they walked back to CID headquarters before returning to London. Just before they left Hammersley said to him, 'What about a sweetener for the informer?. He's had nothing yet.'

He said he called Superintendent Moody out of the car and said, 'Mr. Hammersley has spoken to me about a sweetener for his informant – perhaps you will deal with that?' Hammersley then repeated his words to Moody, who said he would see what he could do about it.

On August 31st Insp Wright said he came back to Brighton and went to 155 Preston Road to execute a search warrant but found the doors locked. Then other officers arrived with Ernest Waite, who unlocked the door. On September 3rd he again came to Brighton with Superintendent Moody and he said he was present when the latter saw Ridge. On September 12th, when again in Brighton, the inspector said he saw Hammersley that evening in the Seven Stars public house. Hammersley appeared anxious to know what had occurred at the interview between Superintendent Moody and Mr. Ridge.

'I said Mr. Moody said nothing at all to Hammersley's detriment and he replied, "I'm relieved to hear that." '

Wright added that he told Hammersley, 'He could have said a great deal but did not do so.' Hammersley did not reply.

'I said, "Our primary job down here in Brighton is to obtain as much information as possible to bring to a successful conclusion a most serious theft, if at all possible." Hammersley answered by saying, "That's what we're here for." I said, "If that's so I can't understand why we can't get some real help so we can get cracking. I have never known a job stand still so long." Hammersley said, "I'm doing my best." '

At this stage Mr. David Peck, for Hammersley, asked to see the notebook to which Insp Wright had referred during his evidence. He sat down with it for several minutes, turning back the pages several times. Then he rose from his seat and addressed the inspector again.

'Were these notes in this book written all at the same time?'

'No, they were written all in the same pen at different intervals, each night I wrote up the book.'

'Does it start on October 3rd 1957?'

'That is following on from the previous book.'

'May I take it that all the entries in this book were written after October 3rd 1957?'

'Just look at the front page. It means it follows on from the previous book which commenced on July 22nd.'

Mr. Peck persisted, asking in a slightly louder voice, 'Does that mean you commenced that book on October 3rd?'

'Yes.'

As Insp Wright looked at the book, Mr. Peck rapped out, 'Put that book away.' Then he went on, 'When you say you commenced on October 3rd, do you mean you commenced writing in this book on October 3rd?'

'Yes.'

'Does that mean you started writing that book on October 3rd? The entries in that book relate to a date before October 3rd, don't they? Do they relate to events before October?'

'Yes.'

'You told the court earlier you wrote events up each evening as they occurred?'

Yes.'

'Did you write events up in that book the same evening as they occurred?'

'No.'

Mr Peck, now standing with a triumphant smile on his face, said, 'Can you explain why you told the magistrates you did?'

'What I said,' the inspector replied calmly, 'was I made my book up each evening.'

After he was questioned about whether he had made some notes during the early stages of the proceedings while he was actually talking with police officers, Insp Wright said, 'You don't make notes at such an early stage when police officers are on an enquiry together.'

He said that he made notes on pieces of paper and afterwards copied them into a copy book.

'If this case goes for trial,' Mr Peck asked, 'will you be certain to have your notebooks available for the trial?'

'Yes, I will.'

Insp Wright now left the witness box, to be followed by Detective Inspector Roland Hendy of Brighton Railway Police.

He said that on August 20th he saw Hammersley and Heath in his office. Hammersley gave him two empty Senior Service cigarette cartons and Heath said, 'What about the other 28 cartons?' Hammersley replied, 'I don't want to know, I'm on leave.'

After they had gone, Hendy telephoned Supt Moody.

He said that on September 13th he had been to Newhaven by car, and coming back with DC Cook they went back along New England Road. As they went past Waite's shop, Cook said something to him. He looked round and saw Heath walking down the road carrying a basket.

DC Cook was himself the next witness. During the previous day's hearing had been described as an undercover railway police officer. He said that on August 30th he took up a position where he could see 155 Preston Road. At about midday he saw a private car, index number LXE 861, go into the drive. There were two men in it and they got out and went into the front entrance of the house. They were not carrying anything going in, but when they came out each man carried a cardboard carton tied with string.

At this point two large cardboard Senior Service cartons were held up in court and DC Cook was asked if they were similar to those he saw carried out of the house. He said, 'No, sir, they were slightly smaller.'

He said each man placed a carton in the boot of the car and they drove off. He followed them to Argyle Road, where the car stopped. The man in the passenger seat got out and went to the boot and took the cartons out and carried them to 37 New England Road – G. E. Spencer's confectionery and tobacconists shop.

On September 13th he went with Det Insp Hendy to Newhaven and as they came back in the car he saw Heath as he was just leaving Waite's shop.

DC Dennis Andrew Ward of the British Transport Commission Police, stationed at Brighton, was the next witness. He said that at about 3 o'clock on the afternoon of August 31st he saw a grey unpolished Standard Vanguard motor car travelling from Preston Circus up New England Road and into New England Street. He recognised the driver as Hammersley.

He was followed into the witness box by Mrs. Sheila Swaby. There was a slight pause before she entered the courtroom and went into the witness box. Mrs. Swaby, plump and auburn haired, wore a grey coat and dark sun glasses. She was allowed to sit down in the witness box and to write down her address on a piece of paper. Mr Gerald Howard, representing the Crown, asked, her, 'Are you the wife of James Thomas Swaby?'

'Yes,'

'Is he at present serving a sentence of five years' imprisonment in Wandsworth?'

'Yes, he is.'

'In May of this year were you living at Gloucester Terrace W2 with your husband?'

'Yes, I was.'

'In May, was your husband arrested?'

'Yes, he was.'

'Did you discover he had been taken to Brighton police station?''

'Yes, I did. I don't really remember the date when I went down there.'

'Did you later on go to see your husband in prison at Lewes?'

'I did.'

'About how long before you went to Lewes, did you go to Brighton police station?'

'About one hour before, on the same day.'

'When you got to the police station at Brighton whom did you see there?'

'I saw the gentleman sitting over there, the one in the grey suit.' Here Mrs. Swaby, pointing her finger, indicated Sergeant Heath.

'Had you got some furniture in a flat in Brighton?'

'I had.'

'Did you have some conversation with Sergeant Heath about that?'

'Yes, I did.'

'At this time your husband was in prison?'

'That's right.'

'Did you want to go and see him if you could?'

'Yes, I did. That was my purpose of going down there.'

'Did you ask Heath anything?'

'I asked him if it would be possible to see my husband. He said No, it wasn't.'

'Did you ask why not?'

'Yes, I did.'

'What was the answer to that?'

'He said it was a lot of trouble to see a prisoner on remand in Lewes Prison. He said that even he, being a police officer, had to take a letter from his governor to the governor of Lewes Prison to see him.'

'After he had said that, did you ask him anything?'

'Well, I had some other conversation with him. I can't remember what it was about. Then I asked him what my husband's chances were. He said he would do his best for him. Then he asked me how I was fixed for £50. I said I would have to speak to my husband.'

'Had you got your father waiting outside for you?'

'Yes.'

'Did you go to Lewes prison and see your husband?'

'Yes.'

'Did you go to Brighton Court when your husband went there to be sentenced?'

'Yes I did.'

Mrs. Swaby said she was unable to raise the £50. She said that after her husband had been sentenced to five years, Heath said to her, 'You see now what has happened. You didn't look after me so I didn't look after you.' This was about an hour after her husband had been sentenced.

'I told him he was no good.'

Mr. Cyril Wheeler (for Heath), rose from his seat to start his cross-examination. Answering his first question, Mrs. Swaby said that it was around lunch-time when her husband was sentenced and about 2.50 pm when she went back and saw Heath. The conversation she had with Heath took place downstairs where the cells were, near the door. Nobody else was present.

'Did you know your husband had a long criminal record?'

'Oh yes, I did.'

'Is it right you have 50 convictions for soliciting?'

'Yes, that's right.'

She then left the witness box.

The next witness was her husband, James Swaby. He was wearing glasses and a trench style raincoat. He stood almost erect and removed his glasses before beginning his evidence, glancing around the court before answering a question put to him by Mr. Maxwell Turner.

He agreed that he had a number of previous convictions and was at present serving a sentence of five years' imprisonment for housebreaking. He said that one other offence was taken into consideration and the sentence dated from June 20th that year. He had been arrested in London in May, and before being brought to Brighton by Detective Constable Hovey and another officer he was searched at Paddington police station.

Swaby said that he concealed two £5 notes in the hem of his raincoat. They were not found while he was remanded in Lewes prison. Later he asked Heath if he could help him straighten out a maintenance case.

'I also mentioned some of the charges I was convicted of,' he added, 'and asked if they could be straightened out as they were wrong. I later said, "Can you help me?" He said, "It's up to you." '

Swaby said he then took out the two £5 notes from his coat and gave them to Heath.

That ended the day's court hearing, and the magistrates adjourned the hearing until the following day.

Day Nine

Chill winds whistled around the town hall on the morning of Thursday 5th December, and by 8.30 am the queue stretched half way around the building.

The first witness, (the 56th of the trial), was DC Raymond Hovey of Brighton Police, based in the CID. He told the court that he saw James Swaby detained at Paddington on May 22nd. At Brighton the following day he was remanded in custody until May 28th. On the day before he appeared in court again, he took Heath down to see Swaby and introduced him as the officer in the case.

'Swaby was in the cells and Heath in the corridor outside the cells,' he said. 'Heath spoke to Swaby and while they were talking I left them.'

DC Hovey and Heath later saw Swaby at Lewes Prison, where he was on remand. Swaby was eligible for 'preventive detention,' and the officers went there to serve the necessary forms. There was some talk about Swaby's antecedent history, and some points to clear up about Swaby's occupation. Swaby, who had previous convictions, was very worried about his last conviction for living on immoral earnings.

'Who was the officer who gave Swaby's previous convictions and character to the court?' asked Gerald Howard for the prosecution.

'Sergeant Heath.'

Constable Hovey said that at Lewes Prison he heard Heath say something to Swaby.

'I can't remember the exact words, but he said something to the effect that for a "pony" he would see what could be done about Swaby's last conviction.'

DC Hovey added that he took no part in this conversation, and he left the prison with Heath.

On June 20th 1957 he was at Brighton Quarter Sessions when Swaby appeared for trial.

'I saw Mrs. Swaby there, and I took her to see her husband and let her have a few moments conversation with him.'

After that, he took Mrs. Swaby into the court and put her into a seat. He also went into court and sat next to Heath.

'While I was sitting there next to him he said to me, "Go outside and take Mrs. Swaby with you and see if she has brought me anything." '

DC Hovey said he was junior to Heath: he did what Heath told him. Mrs Swaby had nothing for Heath and he went back into the court and told Heath so. Heath told him, 'Go outside again and tell her its no use backing a horse after the off.'

Hovey added, 'Sergeant Heath did mention Mrs. Swaby had come with friends. He told me he knew she had come with friends and she was to ask them if they could help her. I took Mrs. Swaby outside again. I told her what Heath had said to me. I then went back again into court. I said to him that she had told me it was hopeless or useless. She said she had only a couple of pounds for her fare.'

After that, he said, Swaby's case came on. He pleaded guilty to an amended indictment. Heath gave his antecedent history and previous convictions. He read all his previous convictions and particularly the last one – the one about which Swaby had been worried. Swaby then received a sentence of five years.

'What sort of condition was Mrs. Swaby in?'

'She was very upset. I helped to carry her out. She had to be half-carried and was very distressed.'

Mrs. Swaby had come back to the police station at about 2.30 pm, but he was not present.

In answer to a question from Cyril Wheeler, representing Heath, DC Hovey agreed that he was the officer mainly responsible for the investigation of the Swaby case, while Heath was the detective sergeant in charge.

'One of Swaby's offences related to property stolen from the Caxton Arms public house?'

'Yes.'

'Did you know that Heath was friendly with the licensee of the Caxton Arms in North Gardens?'

'Yes.'

'Did you know that Heath was anxious to recover as much of the stolen property as he possibly could?'

'Yes.'

'When a prisoner asks what he can do to help himself, is it the practice to say, "Well it's up to you," meaning it's up to him to co-operate with the police?'

'That is said, but it's up to the court, isn't it?'

'Is it usual?'

'To help us recover the property, yes.'

'Is it a fact that in this case very little of the stolen property was in fact recovered?'

'That's true.'

DC Hovey said that when he took Swaby to Brighton police station he made a routine search of his clothing. He looked through the pockets of his coat and trousers. The Metropolitan Police had searched him when they arrested him and he just took possession of his property and valuables.

'Did you go over him with your hands?'

'I did.'

'Did you feel all over him with your hands to see if he had anything concealed? That's the object of it, isn't it?'

'Yes.'

'Could you find anything?'

'Nothing.'

Constable Hovey agreed that when a man appeared at quarter sessions it was normal practice for the sergeant in charge of the case to give antecedents and previous convictions. He also agreed that a copy of these antecedents and previous convictions was furnished to the court for the use of the recorder.

The list of antecedents and previous convictions, he said, was prepared by the officer in charge of the case, under the supervision of the detective sergeant in charge.

Mr. Wheeler asked if, in that particular case, DC Hovey had prepared the document and submitted it to Heath for verification. He said he had. He agreed that it was the usual practice for the detective sergeant in charge to submit the document to the superintendent for him to check, and that procedure was followed in this case.

There followed a series of dramatic questions and answers which electrified the packed courtroom.

'Officer, I want to ask you about the occasion when reference was made to a "pony". That, I think was at Lewes Prison?'

'That's right.'

'Do you keep a notebook?'

'Yes.'

'I would like to know the date of that visit to Lewes Prison. Can you give that?'

'I can give it by reference to my diary. I made no entry in my notebook.'

Mr. Wheeler said they knew that the alleged conversation about the 'pony' was before June 20th, when Swaby appeared at quarter sessions, and he asked Hovey if he could tell them about how long before. He replied that he thought it was about four days before. He said his notebook contained no entry whatsoever about the visit to Lewes prison with Heath.

'A conversation of this nature you thought too insignificant to record in your notebook?'

'I was alarmed. I was disgusted, in fact – but I think it is a case of misplaced loyalty.'

'When did you report it?'

'I did not report it.'

'When did you first make a statement about it?'

'It was on October 31st. I received an anonymous letter.'

'The 31st was after the "probe," if I can call it that, had started?'

'Yes.'

'Turning to the conversation of June 20th in the court, when did you report that?'

'When I made the statement on October 31st.'

'Did you make a note in your notebook?'

'No.'

DC Hovey was then asked by Mr. Howard, prosecuting, 'Who was the chief constable of Brighton at this time?'

'Mr. Ridge.'

'You have been asked why you didn't report this matter. Just tell us why?'

At this point, Mr. Wheeler jumped to his feet, suggesting that Constable Hovey had already answered that question when he referred to misplaced loyalty. Mr. Howard countered by saying that he thought he was entitled to ask the question.

Mr John Bosley, for Ridge, then rose to his feet and said that he didn't know whether the second question had any reference to the first or not, adding, 'In this case we are troubled with the fact that so much has been given in evidence which should not be evidence if the prosecution had not charged with conspiracy but with individual cases of crime. Nearly all the evidence so far would not be evidence against all the defendants.'

After consulting his clerk, Mr Vokins ruled that Mr. Howard could put the question. Mr, Howard thanked the bench and asked, 'Why did you not report this matter?'

DC Hovey replied, to a silent and expectant courtroom, 'I didn't sir, because I thought to do so might have had unpleasant effects on my career because I knew that Mr. Ridge held Sergeant Heath in very high esteem as a CID officer.'

Soon after this reply DC Hovey left the witness box.

The next witness was another Brighton police officer, PC Frank Knight.

In answer to a question put by Mr. Howard, he said that during this year he had been employed from time to time on plain clothes duties. These included keeping observations on betting houses. He said that he knew the Lonsdale Club at 75, West Street, Brighton, which was known as the Burlesque Club and by the type of people who used it as Sammy's Place. He had kept observation on it a number of times.

On June 4th, he said, he was on duty from 6 pm till 2 am with PC Tullett. When he booked on duty he got a message that Heath wanted to see him in the CID room. He said that at first both officers saw Heath, and afterwards he went into the office alone. PC Tullett stayed outside and the door was closed.

'Did he say something to you?'

'Yes.'

At this point Cyril Chapman, representing Bellson, jumped to his feet and urged the magistrates that any statement which the witness might now make should not be considered evidence against Mr. Bellson.

A legal argument then took place between Mr. Chapman and Mr. Howard, and the chairman, Mr. Vokins, interjected by saying, 'We will hear the evidence.'

Mr. Howard then asked PC Knight, 'When you got into the sergeant's room did Heath say something to you?'

'Yes, he said, "Are you interested in earning a tenner a week?" I asked him what he meant.'

He said the suggestion had come from Hammersley. Sammy would pay him a tenner a week just to keep him informed when his club was going to be 'done'.

'I told him that I wasn't interested, and he said that it would be all right: "Your job won't fall flat, and you won't be in the cart because the frequenters will be there." I again told him I wasn't interested and he then said, "All right, it's up to you. I was to get a fiver out of it for fixing it up, but that won't break me. I have my other fiddles, you know that!" '

PC Knight said he did not recall his reply to this. When he got outside he spoke to PC Tullett about the conversation. He said Heath impressed upon him not to tell anybody about the conversation. As he was about to leave the sergeant's office, Heath said to him, 'If Vernon [PC Tullett] wants to know about it, say its about Weaver being in and out of West Street.'

'Do you personally know of any fiddles that Heath was talking about.'

'I don't know, no.'

Cyril Chapman, for Bellson, slowly rose to his feet, his eyes firmly fixed on PC Knight. He paused for a second, then asked if he thought it was true that Bellson's club had been raided five times.

'I think it has been raided three times in West Street and twice when he had a club on the seafront.'

"TENNER A WEEK" OFFER BY HEATH, SAYS P.c.

" Not Interested " in Warning Club Owner of Raids : Bookmaker's Advice

DAILY TELEGRAPH REPORTER

P.c. FRANK KENNETH KNIGHT, of the Brighton police force, said in evidence in the Brighton conspiracy case yesterday that Det. Sgt. HEATH, one of the accused officers, asked him if he was " interested in earning a tenner a week " by informing a man " when his club is going to be done."

The constable said he had kept watch in plain clothes a number of times on the Lonsdale Club in West Street, Brighton, which had been known as the Burlesque and, to those who went there as " Sammy's Place." Sgt. Heath had said to him: " Mr. Hammersley has asked me to [duction, it was in his bar: but it "...... and that Sammy was certainly not to effect protection

P.c. F. K. KNIGHT, of th Brighton police force, who gav evidence at Brighton durin yesterday's hearing of th

In his evidence on Day 9 of the Brighton hearing, PC Frank Knight told magistrates that he turned down a corrupt offer from a superior officer in the CID.

PC Knight was followed into the witness box by PC Vernon Tullett, the 58th witness. In answer to Mr. Howard's question, he said that he recalled the occasion when PC Knight saw Heath in the sergeant's office of the CID building. He waited outside and when PC Knight came out he said something to him.

The next witness was Supt Thomas Hill, the deputy chief constable of Brighton. He begam his evidence by giving details of the organisation of the Brighton force. There were two divisions, each with a superintendent in charge – 'A' Division at the Town Hall and 'B' Division at Wellington Road. There were CID officers attached to each division, and a detective superintendent and a detective inspector had overall supervision of all divisions.

He produced a chart showing the organisation of the force and also a document showing the position in the force occupied by Ridge, Hammersley and Heath from 1948 to 1957. That showed, he said, that Ridge was a detective sergeant until April 30th 1948, when he became a detective inspector. On July 31st 1949, he became detective chief-inspector and later detective superintendent. He was appointed deputy chief constable in 1954 and on July 30th, 1956, he became the chief constable.

Supt Hill said Hammersley became a detective constable in 1948 and a detective sergeant in 1952. On June 30th, 1955, he became a uniformed sergeant on 'A' Division and in June 1956, he was promoted to detective inspector. Heath was a detective constable until June 30th 1955, when he became a detective sergeant. He said it was the duty of the detective inspector to make out a duty rota.

He then produced the CID rota from October 29th 1956 to October 27th 1957, and that showed, he said, that Hammersley was on annual leave from August 16th to September 2nd 1957. He said CID officers made no record when they came off or went on duty, but a 'destination book' was kept at each divisional headquarters. If a CID officer below the rank of detective inspector left the office he had to show in the destination book the time of leaving, name and destination, and the name of any other officer who accompanied him. He did not have to make an entry in the book when he returned, but if an officer outside his office needed to go to some new destination and he rang to record that, an entry should be made in the book, giving the time he rang, the place from which he telephoned and his next destination.

Supt Hill then produced nine destination books and verified various books and records. He identified 101 of Heath's diaries, covering the period from April 1949 to October 1957, and 86 of Hammersley's, covering the period of March 1948 to June 1955. He then identified four pocket-books belonging to Hammersley and 44 belonging to Heath. The pocket-books were numbered 1–45, and no. 27 was missing. A police telephone message book for 1955 was then produced, and he agreed that on June 24th, 1957, there was no record of a telephone call from Folkestone police to Brighton police.

Supt Hill said that 24141 was the telephone number of Brighton 'A' Division, which went through the exchange at the town hall. He said that 21720 was a private line in the CID sergeant's office, which did not go through the exchange in the town hall.

'Was that line disconnected on September 18th this year?' asked Mr Maxwell Turner for the prosecution.

'Yes.'

He was then asked if during the period 1955–56, when Hammersley was a uniformed sergeant, he had been serving under him on 'A' Division. Supt Hill said he was, and that he at no time during that year used him to carry out plain-clothes duties.

As Mr. Turner sat down, the magistrates decided to adjourn the proceedings for lunch. During the break the usual queues formed outside the west door of the town hall. People were particularly interested in hearing what the Scotland Yard officers were going to say: the very name Scotland Yard had a magical ring for many.

Mr Bosley, for Ridge, was first to his feet in the afternoon session, beginning his cross-examination of Superintendent Hill. In answer to his first question, Hill said that the establishment of the Brighton force was 285 officers. Police work was divided into uniformed work and plain-clothes work. Some work automatically went to the uniformed section while other work went automatically to the plain clothes branch. Licensing was dealt with by uniformed officers, and clubs came under licensing.

Asked if Ridge had a list made of 'dubious clubs', Supt Hill answered, 'Not to my knowledge. However, he did have a list of clubs.'

'A list divided into two sections, one for dubious and the other for reputable?'

'No.'

As Mr. Bosley resumed his seat, his place was taken by David Peck, for Hammersley. Supt Hill agreed that the CID kept crime and complaint records. Each crime had its own file, and these files were available at the CID office. Mr. Peck said that he had spoken to Mr. Turner, for the prosecution, during the lunch adjournment, and he had been told that the defence would be able to see those files after the hearing.

Cyril Wheeler (for Heath), began his cross-examination by

asking Supt Hill if it was right that Heath had been commended eight or nine times, one being a watch committee commendation?

'He has had 11 commendations.'

'Is it right that while he was a detective constable he made more arrests than any other officer?'

'I can't answer that, but I am very doubtful.'

Mr. Wheeler explained that he had meant during the last year, before Heath was made up to sergeant.

'I cannot answer that. It might be possible to look it up.'

'Is it right that before he was made up to sergeant Heath made a considerable number of arrests?'

Supt Hill agreed with that, adding, 'As far as I am aware, his character in the police force is good.'

This ended Supt Hill's evidence, and he left the witness box.

The next witness was the first of the Scotland Yard officers to be giving evidence. Det Supt Richard Radford strode confidently across the courtroom to the witness box. He took the oath in a clear and strong voice, making an effort to lay the small bible on the shelf of the witness box. He glanced around the courtroom, as if to get to know where everyone was. He coughed to clear his throat and looked at Mr. Maxwell Turner, who had risen to his feet ready to ask the questions.

He was asked about having lunch with the witnesses Mr. and Mrs. Bennett on November 26th.

'Was this case, and was the evidence in this case discussed at all?' Mr Turner asked.

'Not at all.'

He agreed that Bennett was giving evidence at this time, and that Mrs. Bennett began to give her evidence that afternoon. He said that on October 2nd this year he went to Sherry's bar, where he saw the accused, Lyons, and told him that Mr. Forbes-Leith would like to see him. Lyons said to him, 'What's your name and where have you come from? I know you're not a local police officer.'

Det Supt Radford said he made an appointment to see Lyons at 3.30 and went with Supt Forbes-Leith. Lyons said to Forbes-Leith, 'Yes, I know you. I remember you from 1940, when you dealt with my application for the Bagatelle Club in London. What's all this about?'

Then Forbes-Leith said to Lyons, 'You have probably seen in the papers today that there is an inquiry going on respecting certain matters in Brighton, and it is because of this that I have come to see you. In the course of the inquires I have made so far your name has been mentioned, and it is only right that I should lay the facts before you, in order that you give me an explanation if you wish to do so.'

The superintendent said Lyons replied, 'I understand, so what do you want to know?' Forbes-Leith told him it was in connection with the Astor Club, in 1955, and Lyons told him he knew the place. It was run by Brown.

Forbes-Leith said, 'I understand you have known Brown for some years and have been on friendly terms with him.' Lyons had nodded his agreement and said that he had known him for quite a number of years, particularly when he was acting as a chef in a hotel in Brighton.

'But, what has this got to do with the Astor Club?' he asked.

Forbes-Leith said, 'Is it to your knowledge that the Astor Club was, during 1955, serving after hours?'

Lyons replied, 'Yes, and so were many others.'

Forbes-Leith persisted with his questioning.

'In fact, it was known as the Bucket of Blood?'

Lyons had again agreed with him. Forbes-Leith then asked Lyons if he visited the Astor Club much himself. Lyons told him, 'No, very rarely. How could I? I was a sick man and was ill in bed. I couldn't have visited it.'

Det Supt Radford said Forbes-Leith asked Lyons when he was ill in bed. and Lyons told him he could tell him exactly, by looking at his diary at home. He said he was ill for eight months and did not get up until August of the previous year.

'That means,' Forbes-Leith said, 'you only went to bed at the beginning of 1956, and I am speaking of the whole of 1955.'

Lyons said, 'Well, I must have been down there, I suppose, but what's all this leading up to?'

Forbes-Leith told him he had evidence to show that he went to the club with Det Supt Ridge (as he was then) 'for the purpose of effecting an introduction to Brown, the purpose being to make arrangements whereby the club would get protection if it had drinks after the permitted hours'. In answer to that question, said the superintendent, Lyons replied, 'Not me.'

'Now give this careful consideration,' Forbes-Leith then said to him. 'I am telling you there is evidence to this effect and I am giving you the opportunity of making some explanation for this introduction.'

Lyons then asked him, 'Are you suggesting that I am a fixer?'

At this point, said Radford, he himself entered the conversation and told Lyons not to look at it in that way.

'We're not suggesting that at all,' he said. 'What we are saying to you is that you introduced Superintendent Ridge to Brown for the purpose of affecting some form of protection to the club.'

'Why should I? Lyons replied. 'I've got a good business here. I don't want to make money out of things like that.'

'I am not asking why you shouldn't,' Forbes-Leith said. 'I'm asking you for an explanation for doing so.'

Lyons replied, 'All I can say is, I didn't.'

'Are you then suggesting that you never took Mr. Ridge down to the club?'

'I might have – 1955 is a long time ago.'

'Well, Mr. Ridge used to go to your bar.'

'Yes, he's been here hundreds of times, all the CID come here.'

'Well, now you must remember whether or not you did go down to the club with Mr. Ridge and whether you did effect this introduction.'

'Well, if I did effect an introduction. I did it here in the bar.'

'All right,' Forbes-Leith said, 'if you did effect an introduction, what was the purpose of it and did you ever suggest to Brown that a sum of money would be paid to Mr. Ridge for the purpose of giving protection to his clients?'

Lyons was annoyed, replying, 'No, certainly not. Why I? I've got a good living. I draw my cheque each week and spend it and give it away. I have got a good nest-egg. All I want is tucked away for an emergency. What do I want with this money?'

Det Supt Radford said that on October 3rd at 11 am he saw Lyons in the presence of his solicitor, Mr. Cushman. He told Mr. Cushman there was no need for him to caution Lyons at all. Lyons then made a statement.

Mr. Maxwell Turner, for the prosecution read the alleged statement in court. In it, Lyons said that he had been employed at Sherry's Bar for the past eight-and-a-

Accused: chief constable and former CID chief Charles Ridge.

half years. He first knew Mr. Alan Brown in, approximately, 1944–45. Brown was then a chef at one of the Brighton hotels. In 1954 Brown came and told him he had got the Astor Club.

Lyons said he first met Charles Ridge as a customer shortly after he took over Sherry's. He used to come to the bar once a week, usually on Sundays, but his visits had stopped several months ago.

The statement said he had no recollection of introducing Mr. Ridge to Alan Brown. The allegation that he had frequented the Astor Club with friends after closing hours was quite untrue.

Det Supt Radford said he was present on October 10th at Lewes police headquarters when Supt Forbes-Leith introduced Heath.

Heath asked if he might make notes of their conversation, and he was permitted to do so. Forbes-Leith told him, 'We have been asked by the director of public prosecutions to investigate certain matters as to the conduct of Brighton police officers. In course of our inquiries your name has cropped up and I am going to give you an opportunity of making any explanation you may wish to give. I

Dishonoured: a Brighton Police helmet badge.

want you to cast your mind back to 1955, and to the Astor Hotel and Club. Do you know these premises?'

Heath replied, 'Yes.'

Forbes-Leith had then questioned Heath as to the visits he had made to these premises in 1955, asking whether they had been recorded in his diary. Heath replied that he thought not, and he was then asked if he knew Brown, the man who ran the Astor Club. He said that he did.

'During the time he ran the Astor Club, you say you visited the club and these visits are not recorded in your diary?'

'I think I did visit the Astor Hotel a couple of times for a specific purpose, and these visits I did record in my diary.'

'The visits to the hotel are recorded, but not those to the club?'

'The casual visits I made to the Astor Club, and in fact all clubs I visit, are not recorded in my diary.'

Forbes-Leith asked him if the Astor Club was in his district in 1955. Heath told him that it was for a time in that year. Forbes-Leith then questioned him about visits he made to the club casually.

'I think I also made a couple of visits to the Astor Club,' Heath said.

Forbes-Leith asked Heath if he knew Brown well, and Heath said he had often met him.

'I have met him in the street and he has bought me a cup of coffee.'

'I am putting it to you,' Forbes-Leith said, 'that you visited the Astor Club weekly during 1955 until it closed in September 1955.'

'That is definitely untrue: you have my word on that.'

'The object of your visits was to receive £20 weekly for the protection of this club?'

Heath had replied, 'That is fantastic. What protection can I give?'

'You were sent originally by your Detective Superintendent Ridge,' Forbes-Leith persisted, 'to collect money for him.'

'Has this come from Brown? If so, there is a very good reason for him saying this. If they are not coming from Brown, I am only wasting your time, sir.'

On October 25th Supt Radford said, he was present when Supt Forbes-Leith read to Ridge and Hammersley a warrant for their arrest on a charge of conspiracy.

Ridge had said, 'I would like to say it is absolutely preposterous.' Hammersley's reply was, 'I would like to say, sir, that I deny the allegations.'

Heath was told by Supt Forbes-Leith that he would not tell him who made the allegations. He asked Heath if he was prepared to make a statement, and he replied, 'No, sir, I have no fear of any investigations that you are making, but if anybody above me has been doing anything they shouldn't – not that I am aware of anything – I have heard rumours that it is possible that some attempt may be possible to shift the blame, if there is any. That is the only thing that I am concerned with.'

Stanley Rees (for Lyons) got to his feet to question Supt Radford about the interview with Lyons. He agreed that a conversation was going on between himself and Lyons 'most of the time,', but he denied that this conversation had anything to do with the case. When he was asked about the reference to evidence in which Lyons was named, Supt Radford said he thought the evdence was that of Alan Bennett, Mrs. Bennett and Harry Waterman.

When Lyons said, 'Are you suggesting I am a fixer?', Radford said he understood the word 'fixer' to mean a person who frequently arranges matters between one person and another.

'In the course of crime investigation, I understand it to be a person who promises a service for another in trouble on more than one occasion.'

As Supt Radford completed his evidence Mr. Vokins called a halt to the day's proceedings, although it was a little earlier than on previous days. The defendants were again remanded on bail to appear the following day.

Day Ten

The usual queue gathered outside the town hall for what would be the last day of the trial. The crowd talked excitedly as they knew that the senior Scotland Yard officer, Det Supt Forbes-Leith, would be giving evidence today. Everyone wanted to hear about the arrests and what the defendants said – and a rumour had gone round that the defendants would be going to prison today. Others, however, explained that in all probability the trial would move to the Old Bailey in London.

It seemed that just about every reporter and photographer in the country was outside Brighton town hall. Several members of the public were jostled as the photographers tried to get a clear picture of a particular defendant or one of the major players as they were arriving for the court hearing. By 10.30 am the public gallery was filled to capacity. Many of its occupants were craning their necks forward to get a better view.

The first witness to take the stand, and the 63rd so far, was Det Insp Thomas Butler of the Scotland Yard Flying Squad. Taking the book in his right hand, he recited the words from the card in a strong and confident voice. Placing the book down, and glancing across towards Mr. Maxwell Turner, he began by saying that on October 2nd he and Sgt Vibart had interviewed Sammy Bellson. Just over two weeks later, on October 18th, he and Det Supt Forbes-Leith had an interview with Heath in the presence of Ridge.

Heath was told they had a warrant for his arrest, and when it was read to him he replied, 'It is a fantastic allegation. I have said before he has a reason for making such an allegation against me.'

The inspector said that Ridge then suspended Heath from duty. Forbes-Leith asked Heath for his notebooks and official diaries for 1955, 1956 and 1957 and was told that they were over in the CID office. They could see them there. Forbes-Leith then asked Heath if he had any objection to them searching his house. Heath's reply was, 'I would rather you didn't. I don't want my wife upset.'

He was told that he could see a solicitor, and he telephoned from the chief constable's office. Det Supt Forbes-Leith and Insp Butler then went to the CID office with Heath, and took possession of his diaries and pocket books.

'Did you find anything else in the locker?' asked Mr Maxwell Turner, prosecuting.

'Yes, there was a syringe in it. The envelope was marked "R vs Mrs. Brabinger; exhibit no.1" I showed it to Heath and asked him why he had not returned it. Heath replied, "I forgot I still had it: I intended to get rid of it some time".'

Inspector Butler said that they did not take possession of all Heath's diaries at that time. They took between 15 and 20 of them, and the others were gathered together at a later date. They all then went back to the chief constable's office and saw Ridge and Mr. Wheeler, who was acting for Heath. After reading the warrant, Mr. Wheeler expressed Heath's willingness to have his house searched. Mr. Wheeler said he wanted to help in every way.

Insp Butler said that he, Supt Forbes-Leith, Mr. Wheeler and Heath went to Heath's home in Bramble Rise, Brighton.

After the inspector left the witness box there was a pause which lasted for a couple of minutes. The court became quite noisy as the crowded public gallery caught its first sight of a witness most had come to hear. The clerk of the court called for 'hush', and the noise abated immediately.

At exactly 10.55am the final witness appeared before the magistgrates: Det Supt Ian Forbes-Leith of Scotland Yard, who had been leading the inquiries. He was a slightly built man with his black hair brushed well back. He was wearing an immaculate dark suit with a white shirt and a pale coloured tie.

He told the court that on October 2nd he was present with Det Supt Radford when Lyons was seen at Sherry's Bar. On October 10th. The two officeres saw Heath at Lewes, and on the same day, with Commander Hatherill, he saw Ridge in the chief constable's office.

Mr. Maxwell Turner, prosecuting, said, 'I suppose that in the course of these inquiries you and Ridge have become known to each other?'

'We have, sir.'

'On this occasion, what was said?'

'I explained to Ridge that in the course of the inquiries into the allegations respecting members of the Brighton police force, his name had been mentioned. I considered it proper that the allegations should be laid before him in order that he could give an explanation or make a statement if he so desired.'

Forbes-Leith had told Ridge, 'The matter arises in 1955, when you were detective superintendent, and in respect of the Astor Club, which operated from March to September in this year, in the basement of the Astor Hotel at 61 Kings Road.' Ridge said he remembered it.

Forbes-Leith added, 'It was run by a man called Brown. During the period that he ran it, throughout the summer season of 1955, drinks were regularly sold after hours and the club was never raided by the police.

'It is alleged that soon after the club first opened in the spring of 1955, you were taken to the Astor Club by Anthony Lyons, manager of Sherry's Bar in West Street, and introduced to Brown. At that meeting a conversation took place, when it was agreed you should be paid the sum of £20 per week, as protection money to the club to prevent its being raided by police if drinks were sold after hours.'

Ridge had replied, 'That is quite untrue.'

Forbes-Leith said he had put a further allegation to Ridge – that on about five occasions from that date, at weekly intervals, he visited the club, saw Brown and received £20 from him, and that the last occasion Brown gave him money was in Sherry's Bar one morning before Ridge went on holiday to Spain, when he handed £20 to Ridge in a folded newspaper.

'Finally,' Forbes-Leith had said, 'it is alleged that when you went on holiday you arranged for Det Sgt Heath, one of your subordinates, to call at the Astor Club and collect the £20 on your behalf. This he did regularly throughout the summer until the club closed in the autumn. I have already put this matter to Det Sgt Heath, and he denies it.'

Ridge, he said, answered the allegations by saying, 'Well, gentlemen, you have certainly come to the point. I can only say that I emphatically deny the allegations.'

Asked then if he wished to make a statement to that effect, Ridge had said, 'Yes, I am willing to do that, but I think it would be better if I had a lawyer present.' Ridge arranged for Mr. Bosley to be there.

'When Mr. Bosley arrived,' Forbes-Leith told the court, 'I repeated the allegations. Mr. Bosley advised Ridge to make a statement. I took it down in writing and Ridge signed it.'

The superintendent produced a statement which Mr. Turner read over rapidly to the court. In it, Ridge was alleged to have said that he recalled one morning in the spring or summer of 1955, while walking along Kings Road, being invited by Brown to have a look at a room which was being used as a club. He went to the room, casually looked around and then left. That was the only time he visited the club, and to the best of his knowledge he did not see Brown again.

'Regarding the allegation, I have not received any money for any purpose from him at any time, and no person has been authorised or instructed by me to receive money from Brown.'

Forbes-Leith said he then told Ridge the facts would be reported to the director of public prosecutions.

On September 18th he saw Heath and went to his home. He and Inspector Butler searched a wardrobe and in it found four ties. The first tie had the name of the makers on it – Christies, Quadrant Arcade. He showed it to Heath and asked him what he knew about it. Heath replied, 'Brown bought it for me one day in London.'

Mr Wheeler, Heath's solicitor, was present, the superintendent said, and he asked what he had said. Heath replied, 'Brown bought it for me. It's the only one.'

Forbes-Leith said, 'I went to look through various ties and found another tie with the same maker's name on it. I said to Heath, "What about this one?" and Heath replied, "Oh yes, he bought me that as well." '

When a third tie was found, with the name Hummel, Burlington Arcade on it, Heath said that Brown must have bought that as well:

'I would not go there on my own.' A fourth tie was found, and Heath was asked where he got that one. He replied, 'I really can't remember.'

Forbes-Leith then told the hushed court of a conversation with Heath.

'I asked Heath how he was purchasing his house, and he stated he was obtaining it through the Alliance Building Society. The purchase was completed on March 16th 1957, when he made an initial payment of some £220. He was paying £15. 0. 4d a month. The house was valued at £2,468. I asked Heath if he owned a motor car and he said he did – a Standard 10, 1955 model, that he had purchased second-hand through A & H Motors of Brighton in October, 1955, and it had cost £530. He had put down a deposit of £330 and paid off the remaining £200 by January 1957.

'Heath said he had sold it through his father-in-law in March, 1957, through the Lombard Banking Corporation of Brighton in order to raise sufficient deposit to place with the Alliance Building Society for the purchase of the house.'

The superintendent continued, 'There was a large television set standing in the sitting room. I asked Heath if it was his personal property. He said it was. It had cost £90 and he had purchased it on hire purchase through Curry's of York Place, Brighton. The payments had been completed. In the kitchen was a washing machine and a large modern gas oven. Heath said the washing machine had been paid off by hire purchase, but the gas oven was still being paid for.

'When we had finished searching the house I asked Heath how he wanted his wife told he had been arrested. He said he would write her a note, and I left him with Insp Butler doing this and went out of the house with Mr. Wheeler to my car.'

He eventually saw the note, which read, 'Darling, please tell John and Vera. Also let Sid know, Love.'

In reply to Mr. Turner, Det Supt Forbes-Leith said they knew that Hammersley was called John, and they understood that Mrs Hammersley's name was Vera.

On the way back to police headquarters in the car Forbes-Leith said Heath had said to him, 'If Brown is making all these wild allegations I expect he told you about the ring. It belonged to my mother-in-law and I sold it with my wife's permission to pay for a deposit on the car. I sold it to Brown because he offered me £4 more than the jeweller.' He said his mother-in-law bought the ring about the end of 1955.

Det Supt Forbes-Leith said he then asked Heath if his father-in-law was still living and Heath said he was. He continued, 'I then said, "Do you receive any money from him?" Heath replied, "Just a pound or so when he visits us once or twice a year." '

He then asked Heath, 'Have you any independent source of income other than your police pay?' Heath said, 'No, I only have £4 in the post office.'

Asked whether he had a bank account, Heath replied, 'No, I only have the post office account with £4 in it.'

Forbes-Leith said that when he got back to the police station Heath was formally charged and cautioned with an offence under the Prevention of Corruption Act. Heath said, 'I am not guilty of that, sir, but I have nothing else to say at the moment.'

On October 25th, along with Det Supt Radford, Forbes-Leith saw Ridge and Hammersley. On October 26th he again saw Heath, who was then charged with conspiracy. He was cautioned and said, 'I deny that charge most emphatically.'

On November 12th, with Ch insp Millem, he saw Bellson at his home in The Drive, Hove. He told Bellson he had a warrant for his arrest and then read it out to him. He cautioned him and Bellson made no reply. Bellson was taken to police headquarters and formally charged and cautioned. He had nothing to say.

The superintendent told the magistrates that he had Ridge's passport. He took this out of a buff coloured envelope and produced it to the court. He said it showed that Ridge entered Majorca on May 15th, 1955.

Mr. Bosley, for Ridge, got to his feet, and Forbes-Leith agreed that it was etiquette to ask permission of the senior police officer when entering another police district to make enquiries. Mr Bosley said, 'In this case, did you ask Mr. Ridge and was it granted?'

'It was asked for, and I understand it was granted.'

'I suggest that Ridge was co-operative throughout?'

'On the occasions I met him he has been co-operative, yes sir.'

Forbes-Leith agreed that when he swore information on October 25th it was detailed information going to three-and-a-half pages. He said there would be no objection to the defence seeing this.

David Peck (for Hammersley), then asked his first question of the witness. Forbes-Leith said Inspector Hammersley's record was excellent as far as the record showed. He had no personal knowledge of him. He agreed that Hammersley had 11 commendations and on one occasion, in June 1951, was congratulated by Mr. Justice Parker for his work in the Dawes case.

'For the record,' asked Mr Peck, 'was Inspector Hammersley interviewed at any time in connection with these matters by Scotland Yard?'

'No. Mr Peck.'

'Until November 15th had he been told of the allegations against him?'

'No, only the wording of the charge.'

'He hasn't, up till the present time, been invited to make any explanation at all, has he?'

'No, sir.'

Cyril Wheeler, for Heath, got to his feet. In answer to his question, Forbes-Leith said he was quite satisfied that the explanations given to him by Heath about his financial affairs, the mortgage position and the purchase of the house had been true and helpful.

'I think he offered to show you the post office savings bank book and you said it didn't matter?'

'That is quite correct.'

'You described the television set as a large set. Would you agree with me that it is a 14" set?'

'I would not disagree with that.'

'And it is about four years old?'

'I wouldn't know, but I am quite willing to accept that.'

Det Supt Forbes-Leith ended his evidence after 50 minutes in the witness box. He was the 64th and last witness in the two-week-long hearing.

Mr Gerald Howard, for the Crown, then asked the magistrates to commit for trial all the accused charged with conspiracy and Heath charged with attempting to obtain a bribe. The magistrate, Mr. W. Vokins, then ordered all the accused to go from the back of the court into the dock.

At this, Mr. John Bosley jumped to his feet and submitted that no case had been made out against Ridge. He said that it had been a 'remarkably good tempered' two-week hearing, and went on, 'We now know the structure and its foundations, and it is for you to judge – and I am speaking on behalf of Mr. Ridge only – how far the charges so brilliantly prepared and so eloquently presented are founded on rotten foundations.'

He said his submission was threefold – the first was that the magistrates had full and wide powers to stop this case now.

'Many people who have heard this case may have come to the conclusion that no jury would convict Ridge on any of the three charges that concern him. In law, it is not sufficient for you to be satisfied that no jury would convict. I must go further than that and submit there is no evidence on which you can send for trial.'

Mr. Bosley then referred to Sir Hilton Foster QC, who had outlined the case for the prosecution a fortnight before. He said, 'The very eminent lawyer has not been here for nine or 10 days and seen the case crumble as far as Mr. Ridge is concerned. There is not a word of evidence here against Mr. Ridge, or the others, of any conspiracy or agreement or working together.'

Mr. Bosley said the necessary ingredient was to find some evidence that those men were all working together.

'You have heard that one defendant has been raided by one of the other defendants. Is that evidence of conspiracy? Is that evidence that they are working together?' It was just as silly, he alleged, as the evidence from the 'picturesque' Mr. Bennett.

If the magistrates were against him on those two points, said Mr. Bosley, he thought there was still no evidence to convict Mr. Ridge. That an alleged crooked detective sergeant working with an alleged crooked chief constable should tell a junior policeman about his earning £10 a week to give a club protection was 'silly', he said.

They had three charges against Ridge. The first was with Leach, and the defence was obvious.

'If you look at Leach,' he said, 'you see that Ridge told him to keep within the law.'

If that case had come before them without the background that had been built up by handouts to the press and statements to the press that somebody had come down from London and arrested their chief constable and brought him before them because he said to an old man respected in this town, 'Your boy is in trouble, keep within the law,' they would dismiss it.

Mr. Bosley then referred to Waite and asked, 'Where is the corroboration here?' There was hardly any evidence against Ridge in the case of Waite, he said.

Mr. Bosley then turned to the case involving Bennett. Mr Brown or Mr. Bennett, 'or whatever they like to call him', had been 14 times convicted, and his wife's evidence did not amount to corroboration. Mr. Bosley, raising his voice from time to time while emphasising various salient points, contended that there was no corroboration of the main allegations. He referred to the fact that the charge covered almost ten years.

If it were true your chief constable was a crook, with the much-announced arrival and the photograph of a team from Scotland Yard setting up mysterious headquarters, they would not have been able to stop people coming in here to give evidence – if it were true he was a crook over nine-and-three-quarter years.'

Referring to evidence of some witnesses he said, 'If you are going to allow citizens to stand their trial on evidence like that, nobody would be safe because these people from the underworld can say what they like and are willing to do so.'

Mr. Bosley referred to 'this rotten little club', which was one room with a bar in the corner. To say that £20 came out of it for the accused in addition to the wages and expenses each week was plain 'absurd'. He went on, 'If you had read this as serial story in your newspaper, you would throw it away and discontinue your subscription if you read such things as this against Ridge. If you saw this story on television, as a detective story, you would switch the set off, because you just would not believe it.

'If this is not the time to stop this case,' he concluded in furious tones, 'I don't know what that power is in the Act for.'

Mr. David Peck, for Hammersley, said the defence case was that the evidence was 'rotten' and Inspector Hammersley had not been asked to give any explanation of the matters. He was quite prepared to stand his trial.

Mr. Stanley Rees, for Lyons, said that if the court accepted as true every single word that was said in relation to Lyons he would be prepared to accept that there would be an issue on which they could commit him for trial. He went on to refer to the evidence of Brown, and said it was suspect because it was the evidence of a felon.

Mr. Cyril Wheeler, for Heath, said he did not wish to say anything regarding the general charge of conspiracy, but was making the submission on the other charge. The whole case stood and fell on the words 'a half will put it right down here.'

He continued, 'Coming as it does from the lips of Alan Roy Bennett, it is difficult to see how any jury would be prepared to convict a police officer on the uncorroborated evidence of this man Bennett.' There was no corroboration that Heath had used the words.

Mr. Cyril Chapman, for Bellson, said that he was at a complete loss to understand why his client was a party to the proceedings. The magistrates were being asked to say there was evidence that Bellson conspired with the others, not with one but with all of them over the last nine years, and there was no such evidence.

After hearing the submissions on behalf of the five defendants the magistrates adjourned for lunch, before listening to the reply of Mr. Gerald Howard QC, prosecuting.

The court was quickly cleared and the various defence lawyers left muttering and clearly unhappy.

The queues for the final part of the historic trial wound around the town hall as they had for much of the past two weeks. A small scuffle broke out when someone tried to jump the queue. At around 1.40 pm the town hall doors were opened, and the spectators made their way to a packed public gallery.

Ridge, Hammersley and Lyons sat back quietly in the dock, while Heath and Bellson leaned forward and chatted together.

When the magistrates had taken their seats, Mr Gerald Howard, for the prosecution rose to his feet to reply to the defence submissions. He stood erect and confident, and began by reading the conspiracy charge, adding, 'You have only to read that to see that it alleges one thing – conspiracy. And, indeed, with the possible exception of Mr. Chapman, I have not understood any of my learned friends to argue otherwise. They were concerned in pointing out to you that their particular client had no act in pursuance of it.'

He said the prosecution had given particulars of a number of overt acts which had been committed by the defendants in pursuance of the one conspiracy.

'A conspiracy,' he went on, 'is none the less one because it lasts a long time or because there are a lot of people who take part in it.'

He said that he disagreed with Mr. Chapman, who said that Mr. Bellson had not been in the conspiracy with all the others all the time.

'In the law, if you find there is a conspiracy he need not be in all the time.'

The question to be decided was whether or not in each of those cases, the magistrates were satisfied that there was a conspiracy as was alleged and whether the accused acted in pursuance of that common desire.

'And it doesn't mean that all of them have got to do the act or participate in it,' he added.

Mr. Howard continued, 'No doubt the link that binds all these alleged overt acts together is Heath. He is alleged to have taken part in each of them, acting sometimes in consort with one or other of the accused, sometimes in consort with two others.'

He went on to point out that in the first case, Hammersley, Ridge and Heath were involved and in the second Hammersley, Ridge, Heath and Bellson.

'We are saying there is ample evidence to show here that throughout this period there was a conspiracy to corrupt.'

It was for the magistrates to decide whether in the case of Ridge there was any *prima facie* evidence which showed that he took part at some time or other in the alleged conspiracy.

Mr. Howard submitted that it could be found in Bennett's evidence, and he also referred to the remark which it had been alleged was made to Mrs. Lawrence – 'The governor wanted more.'

Asked Mr. Howard, 'Who else can the governor be except the chief of the CID?'

He then referred to the case of Lyons. He said Lyons' statements about bringing Ridge to the club and the alleged arrangement made it impossible to say there was no *prima facie* evidence against Lyons. As regards Bellson, Mr Howard said that what Bellson said to sergeant Vibart with regard to Ridge was 'really a confession'. He read remarks Bellson was alleged to have made with regard to the Leach incident.

'This is a perfectly good single charge of conspiracy. In my submission there is ample *prima facie* evidence that two or more of the accused at one time or another were doing acts in pursuance of this.'

At this point the magistrates announced that they would retire to consider the various points of submission. The courtroom stood while they departed.

It was just twelve minutes later that the court usher ordered the court to stand and the magistrates returned to their places. The chairman, Mr Vokins, announced that they had decided that there was a *prima facie* case for all five defendants and that a *prima facie* case had also been made out against Heath on the second charge.

Mr. Bosley leapt to his feet and submitted that the trial should be held at Lewes. He said that by common law and recognised rule, a man who wanted the trial at his own county assizes should be allowed it.

'That is what the lord chief justice said some years ago, and that is what I say on behalf of Ridge now. We would like to be tried in the county here, in Lewes.'

He continued by saying that the case might last three or four weeks. A commissioner would be appointed for it, and the question of time was not against their application. Further, he said, there had been no time yet for the preparation of the defence.

'We have to digest over 200 pages of depositions. We calculated it is roughly 150 people going up to London every day. Alternatively, there is one person coming down in a Rolls-Royce to Brighton.'

This caused loud laughter in the court, and the magistrates waited until it died down before inviting Mr Stanley Rees to take the floor. Mr Rees then made a submission and Mr. Chapman, for Bellson said, 'It is immaterial where he is tried – the sooner the better.'

Mr. Howard said procedure was covered by the Magistrates Court Act of 1952, and it was desirable, in the public interest and in the interest of the accused, that the matter should be dealt with speedily, particularly in view of matters they had heard some days ago concerning interference and threats to witnesses.

Mr. Peck hastily rose to his feet, protesting vigorously that this was not relevant. The prosecution had already admitted that the accused were not concerned in that matter.

The magistrates stated that they would retire for a few minutes to deliberate these final arguments. They returned after just three minutes, and Mr. Vokins then said that as the commission date of the next Sussex Assizes was some 14 weeks ahead, they should commit to the Old Bailey. The first session of the court would begin on January 7th and a second session on January 28th.

Mr. Bosley said he could not be ready by January 7th, adding, 'We wouldn't even be able to read the depositions in that time.'

Mr. Vokins said, 'You can make your application. You do have time for it to be deferred to a later date.'

Mr. Bosley then asked, 'Could we have some statement from the prosecution, having gained the comparative victory of having this case go for trial within ten working days, that they will not oppose any application for an adjournment on the grounds that the defence is not ready.'

Mr. Turner then leapt to his feet, his face showing anger, and said, 'I very much resent, after the fortnight we have had here, my friend's reference to the "comparative victory" of having this case go for trial within ten days.'

He added, 'The Crown is always anxious to see that no injustice is done. Whether we oppose it or not must depend on what the application is.'

Turning to the magistrates, he said he had no objections to bail, and Mr. Vokins announced that all the accused would be granted bail on the same terms as before, with the same sureties.

This dramatic and exciting hearing came to a close at 3.35 pm on Friday 6th December, 1957. It had lasted ten days and 64 witnesses had given evidence.

The magistrates granted legal aid to Hammersley and Heath, each for one counsel, and so ended the Brighton hearing.

THE OLD BAILEY

The trial at the Central Criminal Court in London opened on Monday 3rd February, 1958, under Mr Justice Donovan, with all five defendants pleading 'not guilty.'

Hammersley and Heath were convicted and each sentenced to five years' imprisonment, while Bellson was given a three-year jail sentence.

Anthony Lyons was acquitted.

The chief constable, Charles Ridge, was also acquitted, but he was dismissed from the force by the watch committee in March, 1958, Mr Justice Donovan having spoken of 'grave reflections' regarding his conduct. His sacking meant that he lost his police pension, and he appealed against the committee's decision to the House of Lords.

Five years later, after long deliberations by the law lords, his appeal was allowed. He received his pension.

Mr Justice Donovan.

A Suspicious Fire

During the early hours of Friday 6th December, 1957 – the last day of the police conspiracy hearing – the fire brigade were called to the Castle Club in Castle Street, Brighton, where they found flames pouring from the windows of the ground and first floors at the rear of the building. The club was owned by William Page, who had recently (*see page 87*) appeared as a witness for the prosecution.

Firemen wearing breathing apparatus found 58-year-old Hilda Skelbeck unconscious on the floor of her flat above the club. She was carried by firemen to the bedroom and passed out to fireman Les Downs who lifted her to safety. A waiting ambulance took her to hospital, where she made a full recovery.

The fire had by now spread to a furniture store next door, catching hold of chairs and other furniture. In a very short time flames were shooting out of the roof of this building, while the club itself was a burned-out shell, its contents totally destroyed.

'Four men were playing cards until 12.15 am,' Page said. 'When they left, one of the staff checked around to see that the premises were safe and secure. There were no signs of any fire found during this check.'

He added, 'I'm not going to cry about this. I'll just look for another place.'

The fire was brought under control after an hour, and no one was hurt apart from Hilda Skelbeck. She later said that she had left her bed in the front room as smoke poured in and had tried to find an escape route at the back.

Two members of Brighton CID attended the scene, Det Insp George Dunstan and Det Sgt Leslie Wiggins. They were accompanied by the Brighton fire chief, Edmund Calvert.

In a statement given to the press at the scene, Mr. Calvert said, 'I cannot say what the cause of the fire is at present.'

By the same author

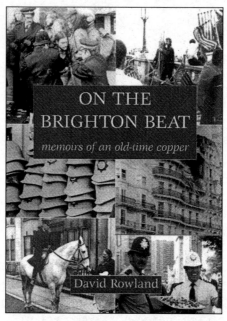

David Rowland joined Brighton Police in June 1958, just after the conspiracy trial which besmirched its reputation. Over the following 27 years, during which the force regained its respect and credibility, he was variously a beat policeman, a dog handler, a driver and a radio and teleprinter operator. He also played a significant role in the local branch of the Police Federation.

On the Brighton Beat is a personal memoir, in which he tells colourful stories about life in the police force in a social era which has passed and is not afraid to make some harsh criticisms along the way. He was involved in many dramatic incidents and met his share of the famous and notorious.

Finsbury Press; ISBN 0-9539392-4-3; £11.99